The Love-Girl and the Innocent

Alexander Solzhenitsyn

THE LOVE-GIRL AND THE INNOCENT

a play translated by Nicholas Bethell and David Burg

FARRAR, STRAUS & GIROUX   NEW YORK

The Love-Girl and the Innocent

DRAMATIS PERSONAE

Prisoners

RODION NEMOV, recently an officer in the front line
PAVEL GAI, another officer, gang leader of the bricklayers
LYUBA NYEGNEVITSKAYA
GRANYA (AGRAFENA) ZYBINA
BORIS KHOMICH
TIMOFEY MERESHCHUN, doctor in the camp living area
NIKOLAY YAKHIMCHUK ⎱
MAKAR MUNITSA ⎰ foundrymen
GRISHKA CHEGENYOV ⎰
DIMKA, fourteen years old
CHMUTA, gang leader of the plasterers
KOSTYA, work allocator
POSOSHKOV, prisoner in charge of the camp living area
BELOBOTNIKOV, a clerk
DOROFEYEV, rate-fixer for prisoners' productivity
ZINA, a typist, Pososhkov's camp "wife"
CAMILLE GONTOIR, a Belgian
SHUROCHKA SOYMINA
BELLA
1st GIRL STUDENT
2nd GIRL STUDENT
GOLDTOOTH ⎱
GEORGIE ⎰ professional crooks
LENNIE ⎰
ZHENKA, who sings tenor
VITKA, the compère
AGA-MIRZA, doctor's assistant in the camp living area
ANGEL, orderly working in the works and planning department
BATH ORDERLY
HEAD COOK, working in the camp living area
1st, 2nd, 3rd and 4th WOMEN FROM THE NEW TRANSPORT
1st, 2nd, 3rd and 4th BRICKLAYERS
1st, 2nd and 3rd GANG LEADERS
FIRST "GONER"
A "GONER" who carries a mess-tin
A "DRUDGE" PRISONER, from Chmuta's gang

Free Men

KAPLYUZHNIKOV, chief engineer in the camp complex
ARNOLD YEFIMOVICH GURVICH, senior works manager at the construction site
VASILI ONUFREVICH BRYLOV, foundry manager
FOMIN, a foreman
1st and 2nd FOREMEN
SENIOR FOREMAN, in the machine-shop
SMITH FOREMAN

Camp Guards

LIEUTENANT OVCHUKHOV, the camp commandant
JUNIOR SERGEANT KOLODEY, a senior warder
A WARDRESS, with a long mane of hair
VISITING WARDER, from the timber-felling camp
ESCORT-GUARD SERGEANT

Other Characters

"Drudge" prisoners. Gang leaders. "Skivers". Actors from the camp's Culture and Education Department. Warders. Checkpoint guards. Escort-guards. Watch-tower sentries.

The action of the play takes place in the autumn of 1945. An interval of a few days is presumed to have elapsed between each act.

The audience will walk from a brightly lit foyer into the darkened auditorium. In here the only light comes from a number of tinplate hooded lanterns which are placed, almost like crowns, on a semicircle of posts right along the edge of the orchestra pit. The posts are quite low, so as not to interfere with the audience's view of the stage. They are wrapped with barbed wire which vanishes down into the orchestra pit. The centre post carries an indicator to mark the dividing point in the field of observation from the two nearest watch-towers.

There are two camp watch-towers standing to the right and to the left of the arch of the stage. Throughout the play the towers are manned by sentries.

The curtain rises. It is an ordinary theatre curtain, but is not used again until the end of the play. Behind it there is a second curtain—a length of fabric crudely painted with a poster-like industrial landscape, depicting cheerful, apple-cheeked, muscular men and women working away quite effortlessly. In one corner of the curtain a joyful procession is in progress complete with flowers, children and a portrait of Stalin.

To start the show a loudspeaker plays a lively melody from a concertina. It is the march from the film "The Jolly Fellows".

As the curtain is raised the melody is taken up by an actual concertina-player, sitting quite far back in the stage by the camp gates.

Behind the curtain one can hear the harsh sound of a crowbar banged against a metal rail.

The camp zone lanterns go out. They are not re-lit until the last scene of the play.

Act I, Scene 1

Work Parade

It is morning. The sun is about to rise. White autumn hoar frost is gleaming on the roofs of the prisoners' barrack huts.

The front of the stage shows part of the camp zone, the inside area of the camp. Further back stage there is a barbed wire barrier where the camp zone becomes the forward zone. There are two gates in it: a high gate in the camp zone barrier, a low gate in the forward zone barrier. To the right of the gate there is a sentry-box made of wooden planks, which is a check-point. Further back still behind the barrier, there is a work area. There is a tall brick building still under construction with a "pioneer"-type crane towering over it, and some portable scaffolding used by the plasterers. There are also a smithy, a foundry with smoke coming out of its chimney and various other auxiliary buildings.

On the left is the work-detail parade area, crossing the stage diagonally towards the check-point box. The area is full of prisoners, both men and women, wearing ragged, dirty jackets. Some of the women are wearing skirts over their quilted trousers. On one side of the gate stands the check-point guard, while on the other side stands KOSTYA, *the work allocator, an apple-cheeked man who looks like a prize fighter. They are letting the prisoners out in ranks of five, tapping the last in each group on the back with a hardboard plank they use for counting. The work detail looks almost like a military parade, with the gang leaders reporting the numbers of gangs and the numbers of people in them when their names are called by the work allocator. Once out of the gate, the formation breaks up into disorder and conversation. Everyone looks sluggish and depressed. The only thing that happens is a bit of horse-play between* CHEGENYOV *and* DIMKA. *One prisoner bends down to tie up his shoes, another takes a final bite of his morning bread ration, a third huddles himself up with cold. Right at the end of the queue come production department "skivers". They stand out from the others because they are more neatly dressed. Among them are* ZINA, *the typist, in a chic dress, and* DOROFEYEV, *the rate-fixer, who is squat and fat. The concertina-player is sitting on a stool by the gate, all the time playing the march from the film "The Jolly Fellows", lazily and with interruptions. On one side of the queue stands* AGA-MIRZA, *the swarthy doctor's assistant, wearing a white coat. On the ground at his feet sits the* FIRST "GONER". *A "goner" is a man whom camp life has brought to the end of his tether.*

To the right of the stage there is one corner of a standard barrack-hut, its length disappearing into the wings. At the side of the hut stands a post, a metal rail hanging from it on a wire. Beside the post stand KOLODEY, *a squat warder, and* NEMOV, *a tall man wearing high boots and a long officer's greatcoat, still new but without badges of rank. Both men are watching the parade.*

On the left of the stage the corner of another hut juts out from the wings. In its front wall is a small door with a pair of steps leading down towards the audience. Further forward still there is a carefully painted box made of wooden boards, marked "Garbage" and covered with a lid.

On the walls of the huts as well as on hoardings scattered over the camp zone there are posters with such slogans as "Work ennobles man", "Instead of the onerous burden it was under Capitalism, work has become a matter of honour, of glory, of valour and heroism—Stalin", "He who does not work does not eat".

One sees the gangs in the work area dispersing as soon as they pass through the gates. Towards the end of the scene they start their work.

CHECK-POINT GUARD: Join arms! (*Counts the ranks of five*)
One! Two! Three!

KOSTYA: (*Loudly*) Come on, number five hut, wake your ideas
up! I haven't taken my stick to you lately, have I? Don't worry,
I'll be there!

(*More "drudge" prisoners rush out towards the parade area*)

YAKHIMCHUK: (*He is at the check-point. He has a slight
foreign accent*) Chegenyov! You crook!

CHEGENYOV: (*He wears his cap on one side, like a hooligan*)
Yessir! Crook reporting, sir! (*Hurries to catch up with his work
gang*)

YAKHIMCHUK: Short-arse!

DIMKA: Sir! Short-arse on parade, sir! (*Catches the others up*)

DOROFEYEV: (*Leaves formation and comes up to* NEMOV) Nemov,
I want to talk to you. . .

KOLODEY: Hey you! Were you in the army?

DOROFEYEV: Come on, sergeant, we're not in the army now. . .

KOLODEY: Shut your mouth! In here's *smarter* than in the
army. Get your hat off!

DOROFEYEV: (*Bares his bald head*) Citizen senior warder junior
sergeant Kolodey! Request permission to address production
chief prisoner Nemov, sir!

KOLODEY: Tha-at's better, do it like that next time. Permission
refused!

(DOROFEYEV *walks away.* NEMOV *follows him towards the
formations, where they talk*)

AGA-MIRZA: Let's have it then.

(FIRST "GONER" *has a thermometer under his arm*)

FIRST "GONER": It's supposed to stay in ten minutes, doctor.

AGA-MIRZA: Wise guy! You know your rights, do you? How
long have you been like that? (*Takes the thermometer*) Normal.
Get out and work!

FIRST "GONER": (*Does not get up off the ground*) Please, doctor, I spent all night in the latrines. . .

AGA-MIRZA: And before that all evening in the kitchen, isn't that so? Think I'm soft, do you? Bastard! (*Makes as if to strike him. The other gets up hurriedly*) Sergeant! I've got a shirker here, says he won't work. What do I do with him?

KOLODEY: Put him in the cooler, what do you think?

(AGA-MIRZA *gives the "goner" a kick. He limps off after his work gang. Another check-point guard calls* KOLODEY *to the right. Exit* KOLODEY. *By the gates a concertina is still lazily sighing. Voices emerge from the queue of men and women going out to work.*)

VOICE: Look at Zinka's new skirt. Whore! That's Maruska's skirt. The head prisoner took it off her when she was posted.

VOICE: That's it, girls. Shacking up with the boss, that's what I call life. (*She sings*)

> I loved a gang leader,
> The camp boss liked me best,
> I slept with the work-clerk
> to feather my nest!

VOICE: Well, that's that, that's our rations for today.

VOICE: Minimum issue, that won't go far. Bloody gang leader took a whole kilo for him and his girl. Little tart, wiggling her bottom.

VOICE: Hey, boss, my shoes are bust. Look, they're bust. What do I wear to work?

VOICE: I'll see you get some horseshoes tomorrow. Best tyre rubber.

(*The work detail is coming to an end.* MERESHCHUN, *a fat, thick-set fellow, comes out on to the steps of the front hut, stretching himself. He is still only half dressed.* AGA-MIRZA *comes up to him*)

AGA-MIRZA: Good morning, doctor, sir.

MERESHCHUN: O—o—h! God knows why I woke up so early this morning. I can't sleep without a woman.

AGA-MIRZA: You did it yourself, sir. You told her to get lost.

MERESHCHUN: I'd had enough of her, the shit-bag. Well, what's new in the hospital? Have they scrubbed the floors?

AGA-MIRZA: I had the men up all night polishing them. They're like a new pin.

MERESHCHUN: They'd better be! And another thing: I don't wan't to find any crumbs in the bedside tables. . . don't say I didn't warn you.

AGA-MIRZA: Valka's going to die today.

MERESHCHUN: What about Matveyev?

AGA-MIRZA: He turned his toes up. He's in the morgue.

MERESHCHUN: No wonder, falling from a height like that. . . And mind you make sure all the sheets are tucked in. (*He looks over to the right*) Now what's going on? A new transport?

(*Behind their backs from the left enter the "goner" with a mess-tin, making his way stealthily towards the dustbin. He is wearing a jacket cut out of an army greatcoat, tied round with a piece of rope. Behind him a German soldier's mess-tin hangs lidless from the rope by the handle. The "goner" opens the dustbin, rummages around in it, picks out some food and puts it in the tin.*

The work parade is now finished, the gates have been closed. The dawn sun is playing against the upper brickwork of the construction site. The work allocator and check-point guard check the count, each with his own counting board. The allocator is explaining something to the guard. From the right enter KOLODEY, *in his hand a couple of pieces of paper, behind him the chugging noise of a lorry approaching*)

KOLODEY: Hello! Anyone around! Production chief Nemov, over here! (*To someone or other*) Get the head prisoner and the . . .what's he called? . . . the bath orderly.

(*The prisoner he was addressing runs off*)

Here now. . . read this. (*He hands* NEMOV *the papers*) There's a new transport.

NEMOV: How many? (*He is reading*)

KOLODEY: Four lorry-loads. Here comes number one.

(*A high-sided three-ton lorry backs slowly from the right on to the stage. It looks empty except for two machine-gunners who are standing inside the lorry, towards the front of it, separated off by a grill. They jump down from the lorry and walk off*)

NEMOV: Here's their ration order. They've had their rations up to the eighteenth of the month.

KOLODEY: That's today. Good! We don't have to feed them. What else?

NEMOV: We might give them some soup. . .

KOLODEY: Soup? What do you mean? Soup costs money. Make sure they go out to work, though.

NEMOV: Today?

KOLODEY: Yes, today. They can chip in and help our figures.

(*The driver opens the back flap of the lorry. The escort-guard sergeant emerges from the cab carrying a stack of prisoners' files*)

NEMOV: But citizen commander, first we have to sort them out: list them by professions, assign them to gangs. Then there are more lists of. . . .

KOLODEY: Look, don't be a fool. They're here in the morning, right? But by evening they may be out in the forest chopping trees. Let them do their stint while they're here. I'm not like your other guards, there's no skiving when I'm on duty. Get twenty prisoners together, one man in charge, and quick march, left right! Otherwise the commandant'll be back and he'll have your guts for garters. (*Walks up to the lorry*) Get out, you lot.

(*The prisoners begin to rise to their feet. They have been sitting on the floor and therefore invisible, concealed by the high sides of the lorry. Carrying their belongings, they jump down to the ground and walk about to stretch their legs)*

Stop walking! Sit down!

(SHUROCHKA, a young lady wearing a bright city hat, sits down on her suitcase instead of on the ground like the rest of the prisoners. She towers over them. Suddenly KOLODEY comes alive, runs up to her and kicks a hole in her suitcase)

Sit down!

(SHUROCHKA sits down on the ground. The bath orderly appears from the left. He is a well-fed red-faced man)

BATH ORDERLY: Citizen commander, bath orderly reporting, sir.

KOLODEY: Good, now let's see. I suppose there's no underwear, is there?

BATH ORDERLY: *(In amazement)* Underwear?

KOLODEY: What about soap?

BATH ORDERLY: They never brought it.

KOLODEY: There *is* water, isn't there?

BATH ORDERLY: Water? Who says there's water? It's turned off at the main.

KOLODEY: Hm-mmm.

AGA-MIRZA: So much the better, citizen sergeant. Won't take so long to wash them.

KOLODEY: You're right there. *(To the bath orderly)* Just stoke up the hot-house, right? Stoke it up hot. How about that, doctor? It doesn't matter if there's no water, does it?

MERESHCHUN: No—oo. *(To the prisoners)* How many days' journey?

A VOICE: Over a week.

MERESCHUN: No, that's all right, don't bother.

(The bath orderly has trotted off. About thirty prisoners are now on stage from off the lorry, which has been driven away to the right)

NEMOV: (*Looking carefully at the new arrivals*) What's your name?

KHOMICH: (*Gets to his feet. He is wearing a bright red jumper*) Engineer Khomich.

NEMOV: Engineer—I thought so. You'll be prisoner in charge of the men's gang. Make a list of names and give it to me.

KHOMICH: Yes, sir.

NEMOV: (*Inspecting the women equally attentively*) What's *your* name?

GRANYA: (*She sits up*) Zybina.

NEMOV: You're in charge of the women. (*Murmuring among the women*) What's the matter?

A WOMAN: He's got X-ray eyes.

2nd WOMAN: She was gang leader back in the old camp.

NEMOV: Why, are you all from the same place?

KHOMICH: Just outside Moscow. They brought in the Jerry P.O.W.'s, so we had to be shifted.

(*The work allocator and the check-point guard have finished counting with the aid of their counting boards. The work allocator now approaches. Enter* POSOSHKOV *from behind the hut on the left. He is small and volatile, and wears a large cap*)

POSOSHKOV: (*Greets them all*) I'm Pososhkov. Ten foot tall and ten inches long. . .

KOLODEY: (*Laughing*) Show-off! . . . All right, head prisoner, this is the way we'll do it. We'll call the names out from the file, and you and the clerk frisk them at the same time. I'm trusting you, see. Only make sure it's a proper rummage.

POSOSHKOV: (*Shouts*) All women strip to the waist!

(*Laughter among the prisoners*)

ESCORT-GUARD SERGEANT: O.K., read the names.

KOLODEY: I'm no reader. You read the names.

(MERESHCHUN *is watching from the door of his hut. The head prisoner and work allocator stand with their backs to him facing the newly arrived prisoners. Behind them all the "goner" with the mess-tin is still rummaging around in the garbage.* NEMOV *stands next to* KOLODEY. *The sergeant calls the prisoners' names out, and they are searched. Then they move over to the left of the stage*)

ESCORT-GUARD SERGEANT: Nye-gne. . . Nye-gne . . .

LYUBA: Nyegnevitskaya?

ESCORT-GUARD SERGEANT: Bloody awful name . . .

LYUBA: Nyegnevitsaka, Lyubov Stefanovna, born 1923, convicted Article 58, paragraph ten, eight years.

KOLODEY: (*In a hostile voice*) Anti-Soviet agitation, eh?

LYUBA: (*To* POSOSHKOV, *who has grabbed her by the breast while searching her*) Get off! You can't afford it!

ESCORT-GUARD SERGEANT: Soykina.

SHUROCHKA: Soykina, Alexandra Pavlovna, born 1917, Article 58, paragraph twelve, ten years.

KOLODEY: (*Grimly*) Failure to inform.

ESCORT-GUARD SERGEANT: Zybina.

GRANYA: Agrafena Mikhailovna, born 1920, Article 136, ten years.

KOLODEY: (*Nodding his head*) Murder.

ESCORT-GUARD SERGEANT: Khom . . . Khomich

KHOMICH: Khomich, Boris Alexandrovich, born 1920, Special Law seven eight, ten years.

KOLODEY: (*Grinning Broadly*) How much did you get away with?

KHOMICH: (*As he is being frisked*) Enough to keep me in parcels, sergeant.

KOLODEY: That's my boy.

POSOSHKOV: (*Takes* GRANYA *by the breast*) What you got stuffed up here?

(GRANYA *gives him a sharp blow with her elbow, which sends him staggering. She moves on and the roll call continues in silence*)

MERESHCHUN: (*To* LYUBA, *who is sitting on her bag of belongings not far away from him*) Hey you! Little girl!

LYUBA: What?

MERESHCHUN: How long have you been inside?

LYUBA: Long enough.

MERESHCHUN: Why don't we, sort of, get married?

LYUBA: Just like that?

MERESHCHUN: Why waste time?

LYUBA: You think I'm a cheap lay?

MERESHCHUN: I'm not trying to get you on the cheap. This is where I live—my own cabin. Just thought I'd let you know.

LYUBA: All right, live there.

MERESHCHUN: It's boring.

LYUBA: You've got the nurses. Aren't they enough? (*She turns away.* MERESHCHUN *watches her for a moment, then notices* KHOMICH)

ESCORT-GUARD SERGEANT: (*Straining to read a name*) Gop-. . . Bloody hell, where do they get a name like that? Gop-. . .

GONTOIR: (*An old man, broad-shouldered with silvery hair, short cropped*). Gontoir, Camille Leopoldovich, born 1890, Article 58, paragraph one A stroke nineteen, ten years.

MERESHCHUN: (*To* KHOMICH) That's a great sweater you've got. Look at the colour.

KHOMICH: (*He hasn't yet got his clothes back on after being searched*) Yeah, it doesn't fade. Can you imagine that? Feel the material. (*Gives* MERESHCHUN *a bit to feel*) It's foreign. You know who used to wear it? The son of a Swedish millionaire.

MERESHCHUN: I don't believe you.

KHOMICH: I'll tell you, it's an interesting story. We were in transit prison in Kuybyshev. It was sweltering, and a hundred of us in one cell. All I had was a pair of shorts. He had woollen trousers and this sweater. "I'm stifling," he said. "Where in the

Soviet Union can I get myself a pair of shorts?" I told him that for a millionaire's son I had a spare pair, a bit torn, but would he like to swap them for the sweater, a blind swap? So we swapped. Try it on. See how warm and soft it is.

MERESHCHUN: I'll try it on. Interesting. A millionaire's son . . . (*He puts it on*)

ESCORT-GUARD SERGEANT: Semyonov. (*Silence*) Semyonov!

GOLDTOOTH: (*He is wearing gay, brightly coloured clothes. He has no luggage. He gets up and approaches the sergeant with a slow, swinging gait*) Do you mean me?

ESCORT-GUARD SERGEANT: Alias?

GOLDTOOTH: Makarov.

ESCORT-GUARD SERGEANT: Alias?

GOLDTOOTH: Baltrushaitis.

ESCORT-GUARD SERGEANT: Alias?

GOLDTOOTH: Pribylenko.

ESCORT-GUARD SERGEANT: Convictions?

GOLDTOOTH: Article 162, Article 165, Article 136, Article 59 stroke three.

ESCORT-GUARD SERGEANT: Sentence?

GOLDTOOTH: Five years.

KOLODEY: Are you going to work?

GOLDTOOTH: (*Drawling in a sing-song voice*) Yeah, I don't mind working—in the parcels room. You know the score, sarge, we don't work on Saturdays. And for us professionals, every day's Saturday.

NEMOV: (*In a commanding tone*) No need to ask questions, he'll work all right. What else can he do?

(GOLDTOOTH *turns to* NEMOV *and looks at him in silence, then moves towards the work allocator*)

POSOSHKOV: (*Shaking the contents of* GONTOIR'S *suitcase out on to the ground*) Citizen commander! Look at this! Books and papers, what's the form? Is he going to work or what?

(KOLODEY *joins* POSOSHKOV, *and together they inspect the books*)

GOLDTOOTH: (*To the work allocater, who is about to frisk him*) Who the hell are you? A screw-lover or something? (*Pause*)

KOSTYA: "Professional", are you? All right. (*Motions him to pass without being searched*)

KHOMICH: Poor old millionaire's son, it shook him, that transit prison. It's an interesting story. They tried to change his attitudes, make him renounce the western world, and his blood-sucker of a father . . .

KOLODEY: (*Flipping through a book*) It's all in funny letters. You're not a spy, are you?

GONTOIR: I'm a war invalid. I was in two world wars.

KOLODEY: You're German?

GONTOIR: German? I don't even know the word 'German'. They burnt my town. 'Boches', that's what I call them, 'Boches'!

KOLODEY: God knows what he's on about. If they burnt your place there must have been a reason . . . (*Thinks*)

KHOMICH: (*To* MERESHCHUN) No, don't take the sweater off, keep it. I've got enough rags as it is.

KOLODEY: Why do you say you're a war invalid? You won't get off work that way, you know. When I was in Spasski camp they used to get one armed men together, four of them, two right arms, two left arms, and make them carry barrowfuls of stones. Worked like a charm.

MERESHCHUN: It's a beautiful sweater. Thank you. What did you say your name was?

KHOMICH: Khomich. Boris Khomich.

MERESHCHUN: Come and see me in my cabin this evening, we'll have a talk. We'll fix you up.

KHOMICH: (*Lightly*) Thank you. You see, I don't complain. If a man's got talent, he won't go far wrong.

GOLDTOOTH: (*To the "goner" with the mess-tin*) You! (*The "goner" carries on rummaging in the dustbin*) Yes, you! (*The "goner" carries on as before*) Listen, I said you! (*The "goner" turns round*) Who's the guy in the greatcoat? The one who thinks he's a field-marshal?

"GONER": He's just come. About a week ago.

GOLDTOOTH: Is he on the staff?

"GONER": Staff? No, he's a prisoner. (*Goes on rummaging*)

GOLDTOOTH: (*Looking at* NEMOV) Prisoner, eh? (*Makes a threatening gesture at him.* NEMOV *sees it*) Fascist! I'll have your eyes out!

CHMUTA: (*Shouting from the other side of the gate*) Production chief! There's not enough work! Men standing idle again!

(NEMOV *hurries across into the work area*)

BATH ORDERLY: (*Enters from the left in front of the hut. Gives the "goner" a kick*) Scrounging as usual? Bastard! (*The "goner" falls over after being kicked, then limps away*) Comrades, thieves and gentlemen fascists! To the delousing chamber— quick march!

(*Movement. Prisoners begin to exit left, carrying their belongings*)

GONTOIR: What's wrong with having books? Books are allowed, aren't they?

KOLODEY: What do you mean, "books are allowed"? Who said books are allowed?

(*The painted curtain falls*)

Act I, Scene 2

The Foundry

(A foundry with a high ceiling. A melting cycle is about to end. Piles of burnt earth are strewn over most of the floor, making it difficult to see the finished machine parts. A light greyish smoke rises out of the casts. A steady drone comes from the fan tube just under the ceiling.

On the right and to the back of the stage is a round, rust-red, cupola-shaped furnace disappearing into an opening in the iron ceiling. A bit closer to the audience and facing it there is an unplastered brick dryer with an iron door. On the flat roof of the dryer all kinds of rubbish are scattered: wires, used moulds, buckets with holes in them and torn felt boots. In front of the dryer is a door leading out to the right.

There are more doors: on the left, the way out into the yard; in the centre at the back, a door leading into the coke and cast-iron store. When this door is open you can see a staircase leading up to the top of the furnace.

On a low bench next to the dryer sits BRYLOV, *chain-smoking cigarettes which he rolls himself. He is wearing a bluish military jacket and a well-worn winter hat with ear-flaps. The workers in the foundry are* YAKHIMCHUK, *enormous and bald,* MUNITSA, *fat and squat,* CHEGENYOV, *quick-moving and supple, and* DIMKA, *who is still a boy. As a team they work briskly and need no words to understand one another. They move from place to place quickly but without fuss. Their shovels, crowbars and scrubbers are all over the place, but each thing has its proper position and everyone knows where that is. They are all naked to the waist, wearing only a pair of torn canvas trousers.*

On CHEGENYOV'S *head is a torn old cap, set cheekily on one side.*

As the curtain rises YAKHIMCHUK *is using a large crowbar as a lance to open up a hole in the stoppered furnace. Cast-iron pours in a fiery stream out of the furnace along a chute and into a bucket. When the bucket is full* YAKHIMCHUK *uses another lance to stopper the hole.* CHEGENYOV *scrubs off the slag with a scrubber. They lift the bucket by the ends of a long pole with a U-shape in the middle and carry it towards the moulds. When the casts are ready* MUNITSA *strikes them out of the moulds.* DIMKA *carries the moulds away and piles them up. The second mould into which metal is poured after the curtain rises boils up, and metal splashes out.* MUNITSA *puts a shovel up in front of* YAKHIMCHUK'S *face.* DIMKA *does the same for* CHEGENYOV. BRYLOV *shouts something inaudible over the roar of the metal, waves his arms and gets to his feet, swaying slightly.*

Enter GURVICH *quickly through the door on the left. He is dark and well-built, his raincoat trailing behind him. After him comes* NEMOV, *walking wearily. The metal stops splashing. The prisoners fill the mould up to the brim and carry the bucket away)*

MUNITSA: (*Swearing at the mould. He has a strong foreign accent*) She boil over once more, yes? Damn her eyes!

YAKHIMCHUK: (*Shouting over the roar. He also has a foreign accent, but not such a strong one*) I told you cones were wet.

MUNITSA: No, they no wet! They no wet!

YAKHIMCHUK: How come it happened then? How come?

MUNITSA: How the hell do I know?

(GURVICH *makes a sign for the fan to be switched off*)

CHEGENYOV: Don't argue, Munitsa, it's your own fault. The boss said give the cones another day to dry.

BRYLOV: (*To* CHEGENYOV) Save your breath. Munitsa's right even when he's wrong.

MUNITSA: (*In a temper*) I say so all along. I say long girders like this, they want more air, more vapour.

GURVICH: Well, why didn't you do it, eh? Why didn't you? Who's foreman, I'd like to know. You, Brylov, what do you think you are, a piece of furniture?

BRYLOV: I do things my own way. I'm in charge here.

GURVICH: Looks like you've over-fulfilled your drinking quota. You've downed a couple of bottles, isn't that right?

BRYLOV: So what? You don't pay for it.

GURVICH: (*Examining the shop-floor carefully*) *I* see, been making sewing machines again, have you? And what about those pressing irons?

MUNITSA: (*Vehemently*) No, we no make irons.

GURVICH: Don't worry, I'll check it. What's this then? (*Points to a mould which has been filled but not emptied*)

MUNITSA: Rollers.

GURVICH: And this?

MUNITSA: Base-plates.

GURVICH: All right, empty this one. Go on, empty it! (*To* NEMOV) Look, you, what's your name, production chief! You're always fiddling work orders and getting in my hair; why don't you get a grip of these foundrymen for a change. Load of well-fed crooks! Every time they do a job for the state they make things to sell on the side.

NEMOV: (*With restraint*) All right, I'll look into it.

BRYLOV: You've never caught us, have you? You've never caught us once. That's a fine way to talk. You're a cunning one, Gurvich. You're too clever for us and that's a fact.

(*Carefully* MUNITSA *knocks off the moulds and uses a poker to extract the metal objects, which are still red, from the earth. They are rollers and thin base-plates*)

BRYLOV: All right, what about that? Thought you'd got us, did you? (GURVICH *says nothing*) Why get at us when you don't know what you're talking about? You keep out of it. I'm in charge here. I'll see everything's in order.

GURVICH: Huh! I know you, drunk for a month and on your feet for twenty-four hours. If your foundrymen aren't making them, how come every house in town has got an iron? They're all over the place.

BRYLOV: Improvement in the retail supply system. Why not? Maybe the factory shop brought some in. Or the co-op.

GURVICH: Co-op? That'll be the day!

A PRISONER: (*In the doorway*) Boss. Telephone for you. Head office.

(GURVICH *departs swiftly, his raincoat flying after him. Once more* YAKHIMCHUK *opens up a hole in the furnace, but this time only a thin trickle of metal comes out and it soon stops*)

YAKHIMCHUK: Well, that's the lot, not enough to go round. (*Points to some moulds*) Those'll have to wait.

BRYLOV: (*After* GURVICH) Stupid jerk, thinks he's going to boss me around does he? This is my shop, I do what I want here. (*To* NEMOV) You see what a reputation we've got in the foundry? Imagine, me, Brylov, letting my boys make things to sell on the side. Never in a million years. We'd all end up in the dock.

YAKHIMCHUK: (*To* NEMOV) Let's go and inspect our so-called safety arrangements, chief. Tons of cast-iron pulled up by hand in that bucket to a height of fifteen feet. There'll be a hole in someone's head one day. (*He takes* NEMOV *out through the back door*)

BRYLOV: (*As soon as they are out, agitatedly, to* MUNITSA)

I tell you, that Gurvich, he's a bloodhound! He's got a nose and a half, smelt a rat straight away. . .

MUNITSA: (*Laughs*) He's too young to catch Munitsa. Dimka, you keep *cave*. Chegenyov!

(DIMKA *runs out through the door on the left.* CHEGENYOV *opens the dryer door with a clatter.* MUNITSA *and he dig frantically into the earth and discover a second hidden layer of moulds, right under the spot where* GURVICH *had pointed. From the moulds they take out some lace-like pieces of metal which make up the frame of a treadle sewing machine, also two steam irons and several ordinary irons. They use hooks and pokers to push the metal parts quickly into the gaping darkness of the dryer. They close it,* CHEGENYOV *whistles and* DIMKA *returns. He busies himself around a pot in which he has something cooking on top of a freshly moulded piece of metal.* MUNITSA *sits down next to* BRYLOV)

MUNITSA: He won't catch me, not in my shop. He's not born yet, the guy who's going to catch *me* red-handed.

BRYLOV: How's the sewing machine?

MUNITSA: First-class! I fix mould. I, Munitsa!

BRYLOV: That one'll be collected tonight. There, the painted one. This one's to be ready by Saturday. Now, how much do I owe you? Forty roubles. And for the three irons . . . ?

CHEGENYOV: We'd like some butter, and some meal.

BRYLOV: There's only linseed oil now, boys. How do you think things are in town? Bugger all, same as here. Vodka and matches—that's all you'll find in the shops. *And* the matches don't light. What the hell do they make them out of?

CHEGENYOV: What about meal? You can get us some meal?

BRYLOV: Yeah, I'll fix that. Just as soon as it arrives. I'll send my old woman to queue for it. But what about that new production chief? Nemov? Who does he think he is, Queen of the May?

DIMKA: He'll get over it. (*He turns on the fan.* CHEGENYOV

washes himself from a barrel at the back of the stage. NEMOV
and YAKHIMCHUK *return from the back room. Enter* GURVICH
*from the door on the left, very quickly, as before. They come
together near the dryer, but their conversation becomes audible only
after* DIMKA *switches off the fan, obeying a signal from one of the
others*)

BRYLOV: You see, there's nothing to melt the bronze in. We've
got some black-lead crucibles left over from the English con-
cession, but they're no good now, they're full of holes. The
welded ones leak. . .

GURVICH: So what's to be done? Our excavators are standing
idle. The front bushes are cracked.

BRYLOV: What do you expect me to do? Make crucibles out of
thin air? You might send me on a trip to the Urals. I might be
able to organise some.

GURVICH: Send *you* on a business trip? Five roubles expenses
and you'd spend the lot on vodka. . .

BRYLOV: All right, fill in a form, fill in an indent and see where
it gets you. The crucibles'll arrive just about now, only *next
year*. . .

NEMOV: Citizen foreman, I'd like to draw your attention. . .

GURVICH: (*Taking* BRYLOV *on one side*) Look here, Brylov,
you're a parasite, you realise that, do you? You're a lousy parasite.
You get fifteen hundred for running this shop, and you grab two
and a half thousand selling things on the side. You think you
deserve it?

BRYLOV: Some cats are jealous even of a dog's life . . .

GURVICH: You don't do any moulding or smelting, the boys do
the lot. Don't you have the time to show a little interest? You
don't give a damn about production.

BRYLOV: It's my stomach, Mister Gurvich, that's what it is.
The other day I had this terrible dream. . .

GURVICH: To hell with your dream, you're a . . .

NEMOV: (*Going up to them*) Citizen foreman, I really must draw your attention to the mediaeval methods being used in lifting metal in this shop. One broken bucket, with pieces of metal falling out when it's pulled up into the air. You think prisoners aren't human beings?

GURVICH: Look, you'd better stop that bellyaching. Don't lecture *me*, do you hear? I've been on this job three years . . .

NEMOV: That makes it worse!

GURVICH: . . . You've been here three days, so don't teach your grandmother to suck eggs. Your job is to *help*, not put a spanner in the works. Get up there and check the construction gangs—up on the roof! Sons of bitches, they just lie around, don't do a stroke. That's your job. We don't need you here.

NEMOV: I'll certainly go up on the roof . . .

GURVICH: Go on then, get up there now.

NEMOV: But I'm not going to stand by and see things going on like this. I'll draw up a report and close the foundry.

MUNITSA: (*Exploding*) Hey, just a minute. (*Pause*) What about us? You close shop, they send us out with shovel to dig ditch. What about my twelve hundred grammes?

CHEGENYOV: (*Still washing himself at the barrel*) That's Munitsa's signature tune! Twelve hundred grammes and two extra helpings.

BRYLOV: (*To* NEMOV) Close the foundry? What sort of production chief does a thing like that?

GURVICH: To hell with the lot of you! *Before* you get your report in I'll write my memorandum, and by *tomorrow* you'll be out in the forest cutting down trees! Here am I, my excavators at a standstill, and you moan about a bucket! (*To the foundrymen*) What do *you* think about it, eh? What do you want to do? (NEMOV *is puzzled by the unanimous rebuff he has received. For a few moments he stands there in silence. Then he walks hesitantly towards the exit. He changes his mind and walks out through the back door)*

MUNITSA: When Rumanians in my country, our factory make furnace for bronze. We run on fuel oil. We smelt hundred kilogramme in two hour.

GURVICH: That's it! That's a wonderful idea! You mean you can make us a furnace for bronze? 'Course you can, you wouldn't be Munitsa if you couldn't. You'll make us a furnace, right?

MUNITSA: Yeah, why not? I do it.

GURVICH: You'll get a bonus, Munitsa, a big bonus.

BRYLOV: Are you sure you can? You name it, he'll try it. Isn't that right, Munitsa? I've never seen a furnace like that, and I've been in charge of foundries a long time.

GURVICH: Now look, you're supposed to run this place, aren't you? What do you think you're doing, sapping the man's initiative? You keep at it, Munitsa, right?

MUNITSA: All right, all right. I make furnace. I make.

GURVICH: Where'll we put it? Over there. (*Points*)

(*Enter* GAI. *He is short but powerful-looking. Like* NEMOV, *he is still in his old military uniform, with breeches and high boots, but it is all worn and dirty*)

GAI: Cement-mixers stopped again, Comrade Gurvich. I can't do . . .

GURVICH: What d'you mean, "stopped"? Why has it stopped? (*Rushes towards the exit*) You keep at it, Munitsa. You'll get a bonus.

(GAI *moves off after* GURVICH, *but* CHEGENYOV *whistles to halt him in his tracks. They come forward together*)

CHEGENYOV: We're in contact with old Igor.

GAI: Where is he? In the cooler?

GHEGENYOV: Solitary confinement. I've got a pal on duty there today. He says . . .

GAI: We'll have to get him some bread.

CHEGENYOV: We've done that. Pencil and paper too. He asked for that.

GAI: What's their plan? To get him another sentence?

GHEGENYOV: That's right.

GAI: Who shopped him? Have you found out?

CHEGENYOV: Doctor's assistant, Aga-Mirza. Found something under his pillow in the hospital and took it to security.

GAI: He's got T.B.! You mean they took him out of hospital and threw him in the cellar?

GHEGENYOV: Pososhkov's giving evidence as well.

GAI: Bastard! They're all around us, Grishka. These bastards are all over.

CHEGENYOV: Old Igor isn't going to last. He's written a letter home. To say goodbye.

GAI: To his wife?

CHEGENYOV: No, his sister. He didn't have time to get himself a wife. They shot his father in '37. His mother died in the camps. They've got us by the throat. What are we going to do?

GAI: What can we do? Remember—that's all.

CHEGENYOV: I've got his letter. I'll see it gets off.

(*Exit* GAI. CHEGENYOV *climbs nimbly on to the dryer and rummages around up there*)

MUNITSA: (*To* YAKHIMCHUK) So what about it, Nikolay? We build yes? We build it fast?

YAKHIMCHUK: You make the promise, you build it. I don't want nothing to do with it. I don't want no bonus.

(CHEGENYOV *gets out the envelope he had hidden on top of the dryer and jumps to the ground*)

BRYLOV: You know, Munitsa, I can't make you out. It's right

what they say—stupidity can kill. Look, boys, it's not a bad life, now, is it? I fix your quotas so you're best of the bunch. I've worked fifteen years in the camps. I've built eleven new foundries and I've always got on well with the prisoners. Tell me one thing you haven't got? Your bread ration's best in the camp. You've got double porridge, double soup. We make irons to sell on the side, and as for your uniforms, I'll sell them for you any time you want. Any time you want to mail a letter, just give it to me. Any time. Right now if you want to. (CHEGENYOV *hands him the envelope, which he puts in his pocket*) There, you see what I mean. You've got your work, and there's enough left over for me. Enough to wet my whistle.

CHEGENYOV: Munitsa's going for a Stalin Prize.

BRYLOV: Honestly, boys, I mean it. I built one foundry on the Igarka and another in Taishet. We've been all right up to now. If there's no crucibles, there's nothing they can make us do. As long as there's coke, we can make a little cast-iron, enough for you and for me. You don't get whipped if you lie down. But once the furnace is ready and the bronze starts flowing, that Gurvich'll be on our backs all day long, wanting more and more. Take my word for it, boys, I know! You'll have to smelt five times a week—bushes today, some other damn thing tomorrow. Everything upside down and no percentage for exceeding the quota . . .

(DIMKA *sets a sort of stand up in the middle of the floor to serve as a table, and around it some moulds to serve as chairs*)

CHEGENYOV: 'Course there won't be any percentage. They'll pay for the bronze like they now pay for the cast-iron—by weight. An iron girder weighs half a ton, a wheel-bush weighs half a kilo. Your furnace'll be the death of us, Munitsa. Forget about it.

BRYLOV: I never saw a furnace like that, and I remember the real craftsmen, back in the old days. Babushkin, for instance, may he rest in peace. You don't see his sort nowadays. Back in '23 he threw me out of his foundry for breaking up the old women's Easter cakes. Working-class for generations, he was, and he wasn't afraid of anything.(*He coughs violently*) I'm sorry, boys, last night I had a bad dream . . .

YAKHIMCHUK: You go and get some sleep, boss. Maybe you'll have a nice dream this time.

BRYLOV: Yeah, I'd better go. (*Gets to his feet*)

YAKHIMCHUK: So what about the butter?

BRYLOV: You'll get it. I told you, you'll get it. Word of honour! Brylov always keeps his word. If Gurvich wants to know where I am, tell him I'm over at construction site number one . . . or number two . . .

YAKHIMCHUK: I'll say the trade-union committee wanted you. (*Exit* BRYLOV) We aren't finishing any sewing machines today, boys. We're going to take our time. For some reason Brylov's keeping us waiting with the money.

DIMKA: That was a stinking lot of meal he brought. Must have been meant for the pigs.

(*Enter* NEMOV *from the back. He looks depressed and walks indecisively towards the exit.* DIMKA *takes the pot into the middle of the room*)

YAKHIMCHUK: What's wrong, chief?

NEMOV: Comrade Yakhimchuk, I . . . I don't know. I really don't know. (*Puts his head in his hands*) We were better off in the trenches, fighting in the front line . . .

DIMKA: O.K., family, porridge ready!

NEMOV: Family? What family?

DIMKA: He's daddy (*Pointing to* MUNITSA) and he's mummy (*Pointing to* CHEGENYOV) and this is big brother. How about that?

YAKHIMCHUK: Sit down and have some porridge with us.

NEMOV: No thank you. I don't think . . .

YAKHIMCHUK: What do you mean? Everyone's hungry in the camps. (*Takes him by the shoulder*) Sit down. We don't mind. We've got enough, we manage.

(NEMOV *almost sits down on a slab of hot metal*)

DIMKA: Look out! You'll burn your pants!

(*They all sit down except* MUNITSA, *who stands there examining the spot where his furnace is going to be*)

YAKHIMCHUK: Munitsa, sit down! Lovely yellow gruel, just like the grits mother makes.

MUNITSA: (*Does not move*) You never tasted real stuff—back home in Moldavia. You should taste the way we make it . . .

CHEGENYOV: (*To* NEMOV) Are you straight from the front line?

NEMOV: That's right.

CHEGENYOV: What did they get you for? Speaking out of turn?

NEMOV: That's what they said.

CHEGENYOV: Yackety-yak. Anti-Soviet agitation, right?

NEMOV: I didn't think so, but they did.

YAKHIMCHUK: All right, Munitsa, we're starting without you.

MUNITSA: What you mean, start without me? What you mean?

(*Sits down. They all start spooning the porridge into their mouths in regular time.* NEMOV *eats with difficulty*)

YAKHIMCHUK: Go on, eat up. Don't think too much. You think too much, you won't live out your ten years.

NEMOV: (*Drops his spoon*) How can a man live out his sentence in this place? How can a man *live* in this place? (*He sits there, paralysed. The foundrymen continue spooning the porridge regularly into their mouths as the painted curtain falls*)

Act I, Scene 3

The Ash Tree

(*A remote corner of the construction zone. On the left is a brick building under construction, standing at a slight angle across the stage. As yet there is no sign of woodwork or carpentry in the windows or doorways. It is the same building that the audience saw from a different side in scene one. It is now very close and more than three storeys high, at which point it vanishes into the heights above the stage. From time to time the flashes of an electrical welder can be seen through the windows of the first floor.*

At the back of the stage there are posts and lines of barbed wire marking the inner and outer camp zones. At the corner where the fence changes direction stands an ugly-looking watch tower made of wooden boards, the same as the one on the audience's side of the stage. Further on, past all the barbed wire, the bare steppe extends as far as the eye can see. Over it hang a few clouds, high in the sky. Somewhere in the distance an excavator is at work. The characteristic screeching sound it makes can be clearly heard.

On the left by the building itself there is a large pile of construction debris. Nearer the audience are about ten women from the new transport sitting on a low heap of wooden blocks. They have already changed into rough working clothes. On the right is a pile of logs on which a couple of dozen men from the new transport are lolling in a state of exhaustion. In the middle of the stage is a large bucket which looks as if it belongs to an excavator. It is rusty and overgrown with grass.

It is an October afternoon, quite hot. The sun is shining down from the right)

LYUBA: (*As the curtain rises she is singing a sad song*)
>There across the roadway, there beyond the river,
>There beyond the river stands a lonely oak-tree.
>Why can't we two join, be oak and ash together?
>There would be no need for me to shake or tremble.

THE WOMEN: (*Following her lead. Without rising or moving from their places*)
>I would move and so entwine our slender branches,
>Day and night my leaves with his would softly whisper,
>But the ash and oak can never join each other,
>So I must remain alone, unloved for ever.

A WOMAN: I thought . . . I thought it was the cranes flying. But it was only the excavators making cooing noises.

2nd WOMAN: It might be the cranes. Winter's on its way, girls. Warm clothes, that's what we need.

SHUROCHKA: (*To no one in particular*) This is the third camp I've been in. It's always this first day that's the most terrible. It's not a day, it's a year. No strength to move.

3rd WOMAN: It's a long way they've brought us, a long way.

2nd WOMAN: This isn't far. Potatoes grow in the ground, no one can call this remote. There's a railway. Parcels arrive all year round. Visitors can come. You wait till they send you up to Norilsk. Six months in the year the boats can get in. The other six you're on your own.

GRANYA: (*To* LYUBA, *continuing her story*) . . . I never even finished primary school, but he was a man of *education*, a senior lecturer. Funny sort of thing he taught—all about Egyptian pots and vases. We even had quite a few of them in our home. He was so sweet and kind. But what was I? A little girl from the village.

LYUBA: Stuff it, there's no man who's sweet and kind. They're all the same, they're only after one thing . . .

GRANYA: Don't say that, Lyuba. You had bad luck, that's all. The war started, everything turned upside down. My husband wasn't called up, but I was. I was a young communist and an auxiliary and a dead shot, so they took me. I did two years. You should have seen the letters he wrote to me—thousands of them!

LYUBA: What did you do?

GRANYA: I was a sniper. Then they made me platoon commander, junior lieutenant.

LYUBA: Out in the front line—all those men . . .

GRANYA: No, that's the point. I didn't. Not once.

LYUBA: I don't believe you!

GRANYA: You see, I realised I'd never be so happy again, never for the rest of my life . . . Then suddenly out of the blue I got a letter from one of the neighbours to say he was having an affair with some slut from the operetta. It was as if a red-hot iron was pressed against my brain. I didn't believe it. The C.O. gave me leave, I took the next 'plane to Moscow. I got there, it was very early, the sun was just rising. I broke open the door and went in. There he was, lying with her on *my bed*. I didn't have time to think. I took out my TT gun and plugged him. Right there on the pillow.

LYUBA: Dead?

GRANYA: He lived five minutes.

LYUBA: I wouldn't have done that. I'd have shot *her*!

GRANYA: No, it had to be him. You see, he didn't understand. Only now I'm sorry. He never treated me badly—except that one morning.

LYUBA: It's like I said. They're only after one thing.

GRANYA: It's not true. It can't be!

(*Enter from the left* GURVICH, *striding swiftly, his raincoat flying after him;* FOMIN *the foreman, a little old man with a big mous-*

tache; and KHOMICH. *After them comes* NEMOV *in his army greatcoat*)

GURVICH: Fomin, why are these prisoners doing nothing? Haven't they got work to do? I told you, put them to work!

FOMIN: What work?

GURVICH: I don't know. Digging ditches, for example.

FOMIN: I sent ten of them out. There weren't any more shovels.

GURVICH: Funny! Why weren't there?

FOMIN: It'd be funnier if there were any. There'll be five more soon, they're putting handles on.

NEMOV: (*He sounds depressed and forces the words out*) Comrade works manager, what quota rate shall I put down for these people? If there's no work for them, I ought to make out a report.

GURVICH: (*Sharply*) Make your report and stuff it up your arse, I won't sign it. We never applied for extra personnel, did we?

NEMOV: They've come anyway . . .

GURVICH: What's that got to do with me? We didn't ask for them. You listen to me, Nemov. Barrack-room lawyers like you don't last long in the camps. Fomin, get that rubbish moved . . . (*Looks around*) . . . There! Over there! (*Points to the far right-hand corner of the stage*) Get these women to work on it.

FOMIN: The bricklayers have all the barrows.

GURVICH: Well, aren't there any spare ones?

FOMIN: You should have given me some more wood. Getting planks out of you's like getting blood out of a stone.

GURVICH: It's the book-keepers who are stingy. It's not my fault. Go and get four from the bricklayers.

FOMIN: What'll they carry the bricks in, then?

(GURVICH *waves him away. Exeunt* FOMIN, GRANYA *and two other women*)

GURVICH: Who's in charge of the men's team? You?

KHOMICH: That's right, sir. Engineer Khomich.

GURVICH: Engineer.

KHOMICH: Civil engineer.

GURVICH: Fine, only I've got engineers here digging ditches. What can I do? We even had a member of the Academy of Sciences. He went sick on me.

NEMOV: He went dead.

GURVICH: I don't know about that. Get your men together and take them over there. (*Points to the left*) Go on, off you go. We'll find you work. Every man'll get his job.

KHOMICH: (*In a shrill voice of command*) Hey, you clowns! You think this is a holiday camp? Get on with the job!

(*The men rise heavily to their feet*)

1st VOICE: What about our three days' quarantine?

2nd VOICE: We're not supposed to go out to work.

(*All the male prisoners and* NEMOV *leave the stage*)

GURVICH: (*He has been walking round the excavator bucket, examining the scene carefully*) Hey you, girl! Come here! (LYUBA *comes up to him*) Are you from the new transport?

LYUBA: Just arrived, yes.

GURVICH: You've got . . . er, a good pair of legs?

LYUBA: Exactly what do you mean?

GURVICH: I need a messenger in my office. You'll have to run up and down all over the building, all over the area. Clean my room and cook my lunch. I don't have time to get home for lunch. Can you manage it?

LYUBA: I can manage anything.

GURVICH: I like the look of you. Let's go, I'll show you what you have to do.

(*Enter* CHMUTA *and* FOMIN *quickly from the left*)

CHMUTA: (*Shouting*) I will *not* put that plaster on again! We've done it twice. And we scraped the old stuff off.

FOMIN: Come on now, don't exaggerate; you didn't scrape anything off.

CHMUTA: (*More loudly*) What do you mean, "didn't scrape"? I demand a quality check.

GURVICH: What's this, then? You keep your mouth shut.

CHMUTA: (*Even louder*) I will not keep my mouth shut! I will stand up for my men. (*Quietly and calmly*) Give me a cigarette, will you, foreman?

FOMIN: (*Gives him one*) What the hell does the chief electrician think he's doing? His fittings are late, and now his men are here cutting grooves in the plaster for their damn wires. They've scratched all the door panels, just newly painted . . .

CHMUTA: (*Heatedly*) We painted them twice!

FOMIN: (*Waving him away*) You painted them once!

CHMUTA: (*Shouting*) You know what this place is? A shit-bin! I know what'll happen—the sanitary inspectors'll be in next, moving the batteries, drilling holes in the walls. . .

GURVICH: (*To* LYUBA) Go and get Kuznetsov. Now!

LYUBA: (*Instantly assuming her new role, she runs off shouting loudly*) Kuznetsov!

GURVICH: They're completely out of hand. They're a lot of drunks. (*He strides swiftly out, followed by* FOMIN)

4th WOMAN: (*Jumping to her feet*) Boss! Let me finish your cigarette! (CHMUTA *takes a final drag, gives her the cigarette, slaps her on the rump and leaves*)

SHUROCHKA: Pig! God protect us from a man like that! Says he'll stand up for his men—huh! Did you see him this morning? Knocked one of them down, kicked him around.

2nd WOMAN: How do you think these gang leaders last fifteen years in the camps? Riding on our backs, that's how.

1st WOMAN: Lyuba's the lucky one. What a job! All the grub she wants, no work, just twiddling her thumbs.

4th WOMAN: You call it luck? Why didn't he pick you, I wonder? (*Smirks*)

3rd WOMAN: They won't look at her either in a year or two, the way she lives.

4th WOMAN: Two years is all she's got left—winter-summer, winter-summer, and that's it.

3rd WOMAN: What'll she do then, outside?

1st WOMAN: Stupid question! Get out first, then wonder what you're going to do.

4th WOMAN: She'll find her way around, that woman, inside or outside. That's the way it goes. There aren't many men around now after the war, but it's always the same: either you have men up to here (*Places one hand across her throat, palm downwards*) or else you don't get a touch.

(GRANYA *returns with two women. They are pushing three barrows, one wooden shovel and one scoop shovel*)

GRANYA: All right, girls, we've got till this evening, so let's spin this job out—two loading, six on the barrows. Who's missing?

3rd WOMAN: Lyuba. The works manager took her to his office.

GRANYA: What for?

2nd WOMAN: What do you think?

(*The women sort themselves out and begin carrying away the rubbish little by little. They move slowly as if at a funeral, taking long breaks at the points where they load and unload. At the beginning their conversation can still be heard*)

A WOMAN: Look, what do I do with this spade, it won't cut into the pile?

GRANYA: (*Sitting down next to the excavator bucket*) To hell with it, just do what you can. Everyone takes their turn digging. Just get a bit on the corner.

1st WOMAN: Is it true, girls, we don't get any supper?

SHUROCHKA: Of course not. You heard what the guard said. We've had our rations for today. It's down in black and white in the Movement Order.

1st WOMAN: It's not fair! They didn't give us a thing!

2nd WOMAN: You stay inside a bit longer, you'll learn.

4th WOMAN: They treat us anyhow they want in the camps.

3rd WOMAN: I hope they choke to death on their salt herring.

(*Enter* KHOMICH. *He comes up to* GRANYA *who is sitting thinking, and sits down not far from her*)

KHOMICH: Well, Granya, how do you like our little camp? (GRANYA *says nothing*) Real "Gonersville", isn't it? But you know what they say? If you need a spoon to eat your porridge, it's a good camp. Gonersville's when its so runny you can tip your tin and drink it over the edge. (GRANYA *says nothing*) This new transport's really screwed us up. I've gone over the whole work area and I still can't find anything to do. We'll have to think something up back inside the zone. I've got the doctor on the end of a string, that's a start.

GRANYA: Why are you telling me this?

KHOMICH: Who else is there to tell it to? (*Pause*) Four years I've been in the camps, and not one single day on general duties. So I'm not going to start now. I'll fix myself up even if I have to mow down the lot of them.

GRANYA: I'm sure you will.

KHOMICH: You sound like you disapprove. You must have more on your conscience than I do.

GRANYA: Maybe so. But then maybe not. Its different somehow, I can't explain . . .

KHOMICH: It's the same as it was in your blasted war. Prejudice, that's all it is. You've shot dozens of people. You've got medals all over your chest. You went round like a general, didn't you? Then you go and knock someone off on your own, and boom! Ten years! (*Heatedly, not allowing her to interupt*) For God's sake get rid of that damn honesty of yours! No honest man lives to see the end of his sentence. It's your first year, you haven't realised yet. You'll see, I don't waste time, I'll start tonight. I do anything for my own people!

GRANYA: Fine, do it. Only keep it to yourself.

KHOMICH: I'll make this camp so nice and cosy for you, you won't even notice the barbed wire. You've got ten more years to do, Granya. Think about it. If we were on the outside I'd be the sort of man who had his own car. I'd whizz past leaving you gaping. I'm an engineer, I've got talent. I'm concentrated energy, *and* I'm a good talker, do you see that? God knows what I'd be if I hadn't been pinched.

GRANYA: What do I care about your brains? What do I care?

KHOMICH: Forget about the war. And forget the outside world. Life has different laws in here. This is Campland, an invisible country. It's not in the geography books, or the psychology books or the history books. This is the famous country where ninety-nine men weep while one man laughs. I'd rather be the one who laughs.

GRANYA: I just don't feel like laughing.

KHOMICH: (*Stroking her hand*) I'll be sorry to let you go. But I'll manage. What about you, though? Up to now you've been gang leader, you haven't had a taste of general duties. It won't take you long to lose that pride and those rosy cheeks. Then you'll jump at the chance of going to bed with some bum for five hundred grammes of sticky bread . . . Granya!

GRANYA: (*Takes her hand away*) All right. I'll drop dead under a pine tree. You've made me all confused. I can't . . . I can't make anything out . . . Please, go away. Go away!

(KHOMICH *gets to his feet, stands there for a moment, then walks slowly away.* GRANYA *sinks her head in her hands. The women are still carrying their barrowfuls of rubbish, in slow funeral time. The painted curtain falls*)

Act I, Scene 4

Works and Planning Department

(*A small bare room in a barrack-type building. There is only one window, in the back wall, and it is covered with a net curtain. On the right is a door made of new unpainted hardboard. One table is set diagonally across the left-hand corner of the room. A sign reading "Works Manager" hangs over it on the wall. A second table stands by the back wall, a sign over it reading "Work Allocator". There are two or three stools, and a bench which stands awkwardly in the middle of the room. It is dark outside and the electric light is on. At the table on the left sits* NEMOV, *wearing a woollen field shirt, together with a visiting warder, an old man in a worn greatcoat with blue shoulder-pieces, bearing the insignia of a sergeant. At the right-hand table sits* KOSTYA *the work allocator, also in a new officer's field shirt with a broad officer's belt. He is never without a cigarette sticking out of his mouth and he looks like the poet Mayakovsky*)

WARDER: Look, can't you? Look! I want short-term prisoners, do you understand? You must know the situation, I'm not giving away official secrets. We're in a remote area deep in the forest. There aren't many guards and they're all like me, disabled, you see? We can't wait to be demobbed. I'm not taking any ten-year men.

NEMOV: (*Irritably*) But sergeant, where do you expect me to find them? It's not my fault, it's the courts'. Nowadays they never give less than ten. Ah, here's one. Eight years. Do you want her? (*He looks through a list*)

WARDER: All right, I'll have her.

NEMOV: (*Writing*) Kalashnikova, Akulina Demyanovna.

WARDER: What's her trade?

NEMOV: No trade, she's a housewife. You don't need a trade to chop down trees.

WARDER: (*Sighs*) An old woman, I suppose?

NEMOV: Born 1900. Forty-five years old. (*Writes*) Article 58, paragraph eight. . .

WARDER: (*Animatedly*) What's that? Terrorist?

NEMOV: That's right, but its sub-section nineteen—intention only. She must have blabbed something out at the market.

WARDER: (*Stretches out a finger to stop* NEMOV *writing*) No, I can't take terrorists. Cross her out.

NEMOV: Well, I can't take much more either, sergeant. I'll be all night sorting this new transport into gangs. I've got to send orders to the catering department and find jobs for them in the morning. Where have I got time to fool around with you? Choose your own people. (*Pushes list over to him*)

WARDER: Look, I can't see without my glasses. Anyway, I never learnt to read, did I? I'll ask the work allocator . . .

NEMOV: He's busy, leave him alone.

WARDER: There's something else, I need a barber. We had a very good barber once, a deserter from Georgia, God bless him. But there was an amnesty and they let him go. It's been two months now and we're like a lot of shaggy dogs, guards as well as the prisoners.

KOSTYA: Barber? Let's see . . . (*He comes up to him and takes the list*) Now you run along to the guard-room. There'll be people coming back from work soon, gang bosses all over the place, you should hear the noise they make. I'll come and see you in half an hour and we'll sort them out, O.K.? I'll want something for it though. Two packets of "king-size".

WARDER: "Ordinary size".

KOSTYA: Two packets of "ordinary size"? For sixty workers?

WARDER: You'll get me a barber?

KOSTYA: Only for another packet of best smokes. Don't be such a Scrooge, you can nick them out of the parcels.

WARDER: All right, but hurry up. The lorries are on their way to . . . (*Exit*)

NEMOV: For God's sake, Kostya, why get tied up with him? Haven't we got enough work with the new transport?

KOSTYA: Look, you're still . . . a mug, an innocent! You don't understand. I'll see he gets all the "goners", ours and the new ones, every single no-good in the place. Then when winter comes they'll all be in hospital, flat on their backs. In for the duration, take my word for it. Let him have them. (*He claps his hands and shouts*) Angel!

(*Angel appears in the doorway. He is a young prison orderly with one arm*)

NEMOV: Why do they call him Angel?

KOSTYA: He flies all over the camp, waving his empty sleeve like a wing. Isn't that right, Angel? Go and get me that girl from the new transport. (*Looks down at the list*) . . . Nyegnevitskaya. Lyuba they call her. Quick as a flash!

ANGEL: Yes sir! Lyuba Nyegnevitskaya. Quick as a flash, sir! (*Runs out*)

KOSTYA: She's the barber. And I'm off. (*Winks at him in the doorway*) It's going to be smokes all round.

(*Enter* BELOBOTNIKOV, *a clerk, a lame old man in felt boots. He bumps into* KOSTYA *in the doorway and before closing the door says in a loud voice* . . .)

BELOBOTNIKOV: Papers for you to sign, Comrade Nemov. (*Having closed the door he limps over towards the table, looks back over his shoulder and speaks in a low voice*) Comrade Nemov, there's a plot against you. I'll tell you who they are—Solomon, Titok, that storekeeper, Rubyan, Pososhkov—he's head prisoner—and what's-his-name, that one from the cultural section. I'm disabled, you see, they can't send me out on general duties. But it makes me sick, Comrade Nemov, I don't mind telling you. I sit there in the office, I hear everything they say. They're only waiting for the commandant to come back, then they'll shit on you. I'll give you a bit of advice: get that camp order book away from Solomon, get it away from him! And don't trust that work allocator, Kostya. (*Points at door*) He's no good. He works for both sides.

NEMOV: (*Coming to life*) Thanks, Grandad, thank you very much. I'll deal with them. I'll roll over them like a tank! I wasn't in the cavalry for nothing . . .

BELOBOTNIKOV: But be careful. They're clever bastards, they might even try and get you a second term. You know, that's one thing they're generous about in this camp, the way they hand out second terms . . . (*Shakes his head warningly.* NEMOV *becomes more subdued*)

(*Enter* BELLA, *a plump, oriental-looking woman*)

BELLA: Excuse me, could you spare a moment? (BELOBOTNIKOV *limps away*) How do you do? (*She stretches out her hand and* NEMOV *shakes it*) My name is Bella. (*She sits down with dignity*)

NEMOV: (*Nervously, still huddled over his papers*) As you can see, I'm very busy . . .

BELLA: (*Taking her time*) You cannot imagine how delighted I am to see this job held by a man of education, by an intellectual, not some labour-camp lout. The best people in the camp were thrilled to hear of your appointment.

NEMOV: I'm no intellectual! I served four years in the army, and now I'm a prisoner.

BELLA: Oh, that makes no difference at all. I can tell an educated man when I see one. I'm from a very good family myself . . .

NEMOV: Can I ask you please to come to the . . .

BELLA: The first thing you must do is get your own people into key positions. Otherwise you'll have no power. To be more specific, I would like to mention the matter of bread-cutting. I used to work there, but they threw me out and put me on general duties because of some *ludicrous* accusation that I was giving short measure. You can rely on me completely. If I get a job in the bread-cutting room, you will have a minimum of three kilos a day, all to yourself.

NEMOV: Listen, I personally couldn't . . .

BELLA: No, it's not for you, not for you *personally*. Of course, there's no reason why *you* should eat black bread. But you can sell it. Or exchange it for vodka. Or give someone a bonus, so to speak. You see, you'll have to *pay* the people who work for you. There's no other way. You haven't been in the camps long, have you? You'll learn.

NEMOV: What are you in here for, if you don't mind my asking?

BELLA: What's that got to do with it? Article 107.

NEMOV: Black-marketeering?

BELLA: What *are* you talking about? I sold penicillin and gramophone needles. Very profitable. Absolutely fair and above board. (*She puts on* NEMOV'S *table a parcel wrapped in paper*)

NEMOV: What's this?

BELLA: It's just . . . a little something . . . to start you off. Half a piece.

NEMOV: (*Without unwrapping it*) Half a piece of what?

BELLA: Good heavens, I said a piece! Don't you know what a "piece" is? A thousand roubles!

NEMOV: Certainly not! Not in a thousand years! Take it away this minute! (*Forces her to take it back. A knock on the door*) Yes, come in.

(*Enter timidly two girl students. They are still quite decently dressed*)
BOTH GIRLS: Comrade director, may we come in?
1st STUDENT: There's something we very much want you to do for us . . .
2nd STUDENT: We've just arrived. They brought us here today . . .
1st STUDENT: There are rumours they're going to send us on somewhere else.
NEMOV: That's right, they are.
1st STUDENT: There's something we very much want you to do for us. Allow us to stay here.
2nd STUDENT: But the most important thing is—we mustn't be separated.
(*Exit* BELLA *with dignity*)
NEMOV: What are you in for?
2nd STUDENT: Article 58, of course.
NEMOV: I see, all right, you can stay. By the way, who are you?
1st STUDENT: We're students.
NEMOV: Where?
1st STUDENT: The High School of History, Philosophy and Literature. Afterwards it was merged with . . .
NEMOV: Yes, I know. A real nest of free-thinkers! Did you know Herman Mednoborov?
1st STUDENT: Oh yes, he used to lecture to us.
2nd STUDENT: What a coincidence! Were you in the . . . ?
1st STUDENT: There were so many students arrested after the war . . .
NEMOV: Sshhh! You *must* be careful what you say, even in here. How long have you got? Ten years?
BOTH GIRLS: (*Together*) No, five.
NEMOV: Then you should be all the more careful. They'd get you on another charge just like that! (*Snaps his fingers*)

LYUBA: (*Entering quickly*) You sent for me?

NEMOV: Name?

LYUBA: Lyuba Nyegnevitskaya.

NEMOV: Yes, I did. All right, girls, we'll have another talk later.

BOTH GIRLS: (*Together*) Thank you! Thank you very much! (*They leave*)

NEMOV: Now you are . . . (*Forgets what he wanted to say*)

LYUBA: I'm . . .

NEMOV: The barber?

LYUBA: The watchmaker.

NEMOV: Is that right? It says here in the lists . . . (*rummages around*) Damn, they've taken the lists. It says in the lists that you're a barber.

LYUBA: (*Keenly trying to guess his intention*) Well, I'm . . . I'm a barber too.

NEMOV: Good Lord, you're a jack of all trades.

LYUBA: But we already have a barber, don't we?

NEMOV: We don't need one for here. It's for the tree-felling site out in the forest.

LYUBA: (*Hastily*) You see, I'm not really a barber. I'm a theatrical wig-maker.

NEMOV: Theatrical? Who are you then? Nyegnevitskaya . . . are you Polish?

LYUBA: No, I'm practically Russian. Except for my great-grandfather. He was in the Polish uprising. They exiled him to Siberia. Please don't send me away.

NEMOV: My dear, I would gladly send no one away. I feel sorry for everyone. Only someone's got to go.

CHMUTA: (*Bursts in dragging behind him a "drudge" prisoner, a "goner"*) Now look, boss, what sort of a place is this? I'm sick and tired of this crap. They just sit around warming their arses...

NEMOV: Sshhh, calm down! What's the matter?

CHMUTA: (*Shouting as before*) They sent us a consignment of boots, but the quartermasters aren't issuing them. Look what the "drudges" have to wear. Go on, show him! (*The prisoner lifts one foot, then the other, flapping the soles of his shoes. They are home-made out of old car tyres and almost completely torn off. Meanwhile* LYUBA *withdraws*) That bastard in the clerks' office, I'll break his abacus over his head. You know who'll get the boots, those skivers of theirs. And what I want to know is, who's side are you on?

NEMOV: (*Ordering him*) Sit down, Chmuta. (*Claps his hands*) Angel! (*The duty prisoner appears in the doorway*) Get me the head clerk. Now! (ANGEL *disappears.* CHMUTA *sits down*) How many pairs arrived? Do you know the figure?

CHMUTA: (*Not shouting any more*) Fifteen pairs.

(*The door opens slightly and swings to and fro a bit. Shouts of "Get in the queue!" and "Stop jumping the queue!"*)

KHOMICH: Shut up! (*Closes the door behind him and walks in jauntily*) What a miserable little office you've got. You've got your own builders, haven't you? Why don't you get them to polish it up a bit? (*Sits down*) I've come to introduce myself. Have a cigarette. They're "Kazbek", the best in Russia. (NEMOV *takes a cigarette and lights it. Without getting up* KHOMICH *makes a slight movement with the box and offers it to* CHMUTA) Do you want one, gang leader?

CHMUTA: (*Without moving*) Get it, Ivan.

(*The "drudge" walks over to* KHOMICH, *takes one cigarette and carries it across to his gang leader*)

ANGEL: (*Entering*) Comrade director! The head clerk says he's busy, sir.

NEMOV: (*Leaning forward and speaking in an angry tone of command*) I said, go and get the head clerk!

(ANGEL *disappears*)

KHOMICH: How long have you been in the camps?

NEMOV: This one? Four days. What about you?

KHOMICH: It's my fifth year inside. When did they pick you up?

NEMOV: Last summer.

KHOMICH: P.O.W.?

NEMOV: No, they took me out of the front line. What about you?

KHOMICH: It was worse than the front line where I was. I was in one of the Ministries in Moscow in '41. Those bombs! It was a nightmare. What rank were you?

NEMOV: Captain. What are you in for?

KHOMICH: Special paragraph seven stroke eight. A lorry-load of sugar.

NEMOV: You had an exemption from the army?

KHOMICH: That's right. You see, it was an interesting situation. They exiled my wife way out in the Narym country. I stayed in Moscow. If I'd gone and joined her, I'd have lost my exemption and been called up. Whatever happened we wouldn't be together. So I didn't go.

NEMOV: What was she in for? Article 58?

KHOMICH: Strictly speaking, Article 7, paragraph thirty-five. "Socially dangerous element". Her father worked for the Chinese Far-Eastern Railway, so she was brought up abroad. The security boys warned me. "Young man," they said, "do you love her very much? Your record's as clean as a whistle so far. We must advise you against marrying her." I should have listened to them, but you know what a pretty girl can do to a gentleman . . . Now she's out there with our child. He got badly bitten by some Eskimos' dogs. Nothing but tundra for hundreds of miles. No doctors. . .

CHMUTA: (*Raising his voice again*) Listen to me, production chief. Are you the boss here or aren't you?

(NEMOV *makes as if to rush out of the room, but at that moment*

SOLOMON, *the head clerk, enters with great dignity, wearing a new cotton overall, smart by camp standards*)

SOLOMON: What's happened? The world come to an end?

NEMOV: I'll tell you what's happened. In the first place, if you want to keep your job as head clerk you will come when I call you. In the second place, how many pairs of boots have you just received, and why weren't they reported?

SOLOMON: (*Very slowly*) We haven't entered them in the books yet.

CHMUTA: Don't shoot the shit with me, Solomon! One pair's gone to the bath orderly, another pair to the dentist . . .

NEMOV: How many pairs did you get?

SOLOMON: Twelve.

NEMOV: (*Sharply*) Fifteen! I'm not playing games, you understand? You will go immediately and get those boots back from your skivers. In ten minutes I'll send you a distribution order for the boots and you will obey it.

SOLOMON: You've got no right to do things like that. You can't take things away from people!

CHMUTA: Those skivers? They're not people!

SOLOMON: First of all you cut the office's extra rations, now you want to hand out fifteen pairs of boots among five hundred people. They're a drop in the ocean! The camp commandant can give them out himself when he gets back.

NEMOV: The commandant left *me* in charge!

SOLOMON: (*Restraining himself*) Comrade Nemov, you're no fool. If a bath orderly wears them they won't tear. If an ordinary working prisoner wears them they'll be finished in three days.

CHMUTA: (*Shouting*) That's what boots are for, to get torn.

SOLOMON: (*Pointing to the rubber "shoes" which the prisoner is wearing*) You mean get torn the way he's torn those? He did it himself on the way here, isn't that right?

CHMUTA: (*More coolly*) You watch it, Solomon. You're too clever by half.

SOLOMON: (*To* NEMOV) It's not winter yet. When the snow starts we'll give them the boots.

NEMOV: The "drudges" will all have caught colds by then. Today's October 18th. It's not summer any more. That's all I've got to say.

SOLOMON: (*Calmly*) You're being completely unreasonable, and you'll have to answer to the commandant. Some of us have been here for years. You've been here a week and want to turn everything upside down.

NEMOV: (*Shouting*) I'll have you out on general duties!

SOLOMON: (*Quite unperturbed, to* KHOMICH) Are those cigarettes "Kazbek"?

KHOMICH: (*Stands up and offers him the box*) Oh yes, help yourself. There is one thing I want to ask you ... (*He catches him up and walks out of the room behind him*)

NEMOV: (*He spends a moment watching them leave. Then he tears off a sheet of paper and writes some words on it*) All right, Chmuta, two pairs for you.

(*Enter* YAKHIMCHUK, *large and dignified, his bald head shining*)

CHMUTA: (*In a hostile voice*) Boss, be reasonable ...

NEMOV: How many "professionals" will your gang take?

CHMUTA: I don't want any of your crooks! There isn't enough food to feed my own people ...

NEMOV: You'll get two pairs of boots, that's all. You can go.

CHMUTA: Look, you think you're tough, but watch out. They'll break you. Come on, Ivan. Two pairs of boots among thirty-five men. It's ridiculous. (*He and the "drudge" prisoner walk out*)

NEMOV: Sit down, Yakhimchuk. Tell me something. You're an old lag. All those years we were in the war, defending Russia, was it as bad as this in the camps?

(YAKHIMCHUK *sits down*)

YAKHIMCHUK: It was much worse. We had no bread—just grain. You mixed it with snow and that was your soup for the day. During morning parade they'd read out lists of prisoners who'd been shot the day before. It's like a holiday camp now. (*Pause*)

NEMOV: Will you take one "professional"? Just one?

YAKHIMCHUK: Those crooks have never done any work, not since the camp started. Gang foremen, work allocators—they just kill them . . .

NEMOV: I've had a taste of them already.

YAKHIMCHUK: They can do anything they want. Stalin likes them. They're what he calls "social allies".

NEMOV: Why are they "social allies"?

YAKHIMCHUK: That's what it says in the register. We're social enemies, so they must be social allies. It's been like that since the 'twenties.

NEMOV: (*He is quite upset*) That's wonderful! You run away from the front line, become a deserter, there's a special Stalin amnesty and you're forgiven. You don't run away, you fight and get captured by the Germans, and you're an enemy. I spent four years in the front line fighting the fascists, and now here I am, a fascist, while the ones who stayed in the rear thieving and murdering are called "social allies". Is that right? Our writers like the "professionals" too. They're always noble at heart, they always turn out right in the end. (*Makes a note on the paper*) One pair of boots for you. Yours is a small gang.

YAKHIMCHUK: It's because Chmuta shouts at you and I don't, isn't it? In our foundry boots burn away, literally burn away. Bits of molten metal fly through the air and burn right through them. You stand on something hot, and your sole's burnt right through. We do our quota two hundred per cent, we're Stakhano-vites. Give us four pairs for the foundry and the smithy.

NEMOV: Four pairs! What *do* you mean? I gave Chmuta two. All right, I'll give *you* two. (*Notes it down*)

YAKHIMCHUK: Fine, you won't regret it. (*He walks towards the door, then comes back*) Look, I'll tell you something. You stay here as production boss, that's all right by me. But if they sling you out, I'll take you into the foundry. So you needn't be afraid.

NEMOV: Thank you, Nikolay. I'll stick where I am for the moment. (*Exit* YAKHIMCHUK. NEMOV *is alone*) For the moment . . . I must be out of my mind. It's like a bad dream. What did I want to go and become one of the bosses for? I thought it was like the army—Officer! On the command, left, right! Or was it just fear of general duties? General duties—it's horrible, it's as good as a death sentence (*Pause*) Only being a boss here is worse than death . . .

(*Repeated knocking on the door. Finally* NEMOV *hears it*) Come in! (*Enter* SHUROCHKA, *as usual in a fashionable hat and a brightly coloured overcoat*)

SHUROCHKA: Good evening. May I? I'm sorry to disturb you . . .

NEMOV: What can I do for you? You want to stay here?

SHUROCHKA: Why, are they going to send some of us on?

NEMOV: Of course. What would we do with the lot of you?

SHUROCHKA: Then I want to stay! I must stay! They've taken us far enough already—me who spent my whole life in Moscow.

NEMOV: What are you in for?

SHUROCHKA: Article 58, of course. Same as everyone else.

NEMOV: A girl like you getting mixed up in politics?

SHUROCHKA: Oh no, it wasn't true! I'm a theatre-lover, I prefer the world of elegance . . . I heard a conversation and didn't report it . . . Couldn't you fix me some sort of . . . some sort of office job?

NEMOV: There's nothing like that.

SHUROCHKA: I used to work as a secretary—typing and book work. My name's Shurochka.

NEMOV: (*He nods*) I can imagine. You used to rush up to the stage shouting "bravo", carrying your handbag, cheering your favourite tragic actor. You saved your money for weeks to buy tickets, because it *had* to be the first night. You bought them from the touts at the door ... I'm sorry, you see, I've only been here a few days, I can hardly ... Why don't you go to the culture office or the clerk's room? Maybe if one of the men there liked the look of you ...

SHUROCHKA: The look of me. Are you suggesting that ...

NEMOV: (*Sadly*) I'm not suggesting anything. Only that's the way it is ...

SHUROCHKA: (*With passion*) Tell me, what is it that makes people in the camps so horrible? Were they different outside? Or were they just lying low?

(*Enter the visiting warder*)

WARDER: All right, Nemov, what about this barber?

NEMOV: We've got one. Except that it's a woman. Except that her job's making theatrical wigs.

WARDER: This one? (SHUROCHKA *blushes and walks away*) All right, so long as she's strong enough not to drop the scissors.

NEMOV: Where is she? (*Claps his hands*) Angel! (ANGEL *appears in the doorway*) Remember that first girl you went and got? The cheeky one? Go and get her. (*Exit* ANGEL) Have you picked your people for the transport?

(*Knock on the door. Enter the two girl students*)

WARDER: I suppose so. It's just a lucky dip—no time to look them over. The lorries are waiting at the check-point.

1st STUDENT: Comrade director ...

2nd STUDENT: Excuse me ...

NEMOV: What's the matter now?

1st STUDENT: We want to go. We've heard it's a good transport.

WARDER: That's right, it's wonderful. Of course it's a good transport. We're out in the woods. You should smell the trees during the summer. It's like a holiday in the country.

NEMOV: It's nearly winter!

WARDER: It's all right in winter too. You see, there aren't enough guards, so we can't take the prisoners out to work. They just lie on their bunks! Go on, write them down! (*He shoves the list in front of* NEMOV)

NEMOV: You'll regret it, girls.

BOTH GIRLS: Oh no, we won't. Go on, write us down.

(NEMOV *writes them in*)

WARDER: Hurry up and get your things. Meet me at the checkpoint. Go on, quickly! (*The students run off chattering excitedly*) Stupid little things! Swamps, mosquitoes, tree-felling—what use will they be? Unless our lieutenant takes a fancy to one of them, that's their only hope. He's crazy about women and we haven't got a single one. He's starving! I'll take that barber too. He'll be beside himself!

(*Enter* LYUBA)

NEMOV: Well, where were you? Don't you think I'm busy enough without chasing you? (*To the warder*) Here she is.

LYUBA: I don't know if I'll be right for the job.

WARDER: You'll be fine, just fine, a sharp little girl like you. (LYUBA *comes closer and stretches out her hands. Her palms and the backs of her hands are covered in black blisters*)

NEMOV: What's wrong with them?

LYUBA: I don't know. They didn't tell me. I'm getting treatment. Maybe its infectious . . .

WARDER: Maybe it'll go away . . .

LYUBA: I've had it more than a year. It's torment!

WARDER: What a nuisance—a lovely girl like you. So what now? If our hair grows any longer we'll weave it into felt and make boots out of it. All right, off you go. We don't even have a surgery out there.

(*Exit* LYUBA)

NEMOV: How do you manage without a surgery?

WARDER: Oh, we manage. When there's no doctor somehow no one gets ill. They just live on and on until one day they're dead. No problem. (*He leaves. Enter* GAI. NEMOV *stands up and shakes his hand.* GAI *sits down*)

NEMOV: Look here, Gai, we've got four professional crooks. What do we do with them?

GAI: Four's a lot. But you can give me two. If you must.

NEMOV: They'll refuse to work.

GAI: They'll work all right in my gang.

NEMOV: (*Writing them in*) You're a bit of a hero, Gai, isn't that so? What did you do in the war?

GAI: You mean, what didn't I do? Gun-aimer in an anti-aircraft unit. Then I was in a punishment battalion, then an artillery platoon commander. I shot down two Messerschmidts. (*Retreat is sounded outside*)

NEMOV: I wish there was more time to talk and sort things out.

GAI: It makes me furious. I remember when counter-intelligence had me inside near the front line. They were tigers—the ones in the cell with me, tigers! We heard stories about the camps and the political prisoners and we thought it must be their own fault—big-headed softies. We thought, just wait till we get to the camps, we'll sort it all out. But now we're here—I don't know. I'm stuck like an axe in the dough.

NEMOV: What are we to do, Gai? How can anyone explain it?

KOSTYA: (*Appears in the doorway and shouts at the prisoners standing in line outside*) All right, everyone dismiss! Retreat's sounded, office hours are over. Production chief's busy. (*Dissatisfied murmurings*) Angel, don't let anyone else in, right? (*Enters*) Well, that's better, they're on their way. That's a couple of dozen cripples off our hands.

NEMOV: I'm giving Gai two professional crooks. (GAI *shakes hands with them both to bid goodbye*)

KOSTYA: That's fine. (*Exit* GAI. KOSTYA *puts down a packet of cigarettes in front of* NEMOV) These are yours. (*Claps his hands*) Angel! (ANGEL *appears*) Run over to the cookhouse and get them to do us some rissoles or something, enough for two.

NEMOV: Just a minute, Kostya. Hold it. Is this for us?

KOSTYA: Who do you think it's for?

NEMOV: O.K., Angel. Forget it. (*Exit* ANGEL, *looking very disappointed*) Kostya, you know I like you but ... but it's quite out of the question.

KOSTYA: You're a natural, aren't you? A real mug, green as grass! How do you expect to live in this place? On prison soup?

NEMOV: I'll live the same way the others do.

KOSTYA: Then you'll drop dead in a week.

NEMOV: Others don't ...

KOSTYA: Oh yes they do! They're dropping like flies. I write the registers, I see them being whisked off to central hospital or else dumped straight in a mass grave. You might as well listen. You've got a good job now, and you might as well listen to what I'm saying. Otherwise out you go on general duties ...

NEMOV: To hell with your general duties ...

KOSTYA: Now that's more like it. (*He takes from his pocket a bottle of vodka. Standing with his back to the door, he pours it into an earthenware mug*) Look what I brought—a dozen drops each, enough to rinse our mouths out. But what shall we do for a chaser?

NEMOV: You know you way around, don't you? Where did you

get it from? (*Drinks*) I mean, it's not allowed inside is it?

KOSTYA: You bum, inside's where a man can *really drink*. (*He drinks up the vodka and puts the empty bottle back inside a drawer in his table*) Aha! I'd forgotten. I've got a nice piece of salt fat. Here, have a bit as a chaser. (*Cuts off a bit and gives it to* NEMOV) I got it from a Lithuanian for moving him to another gang.

NEMOV: Just imagine, I had a whole barrel of this when I was at the front. It was war booty. I used to give the boys a nip every day. I never drank it myself. But now I'm in here I like it.

KOSTYA: You're a tricky customer, Nemov.

NEMOV: Look, when are we going to allocate the new transport?

KOSTYA: We'll do it. The night is long.

NEMOV: (*He is getting a bit tipsy*) I gave two of the crooks to Gai. Did I tell you that?... Kostya, forgive my asking... you're a bit of a crook yourself, isn't that right?

KOSTYA: Do I look like one?

NEMOV: Ye-es. You do a bit.

KOSTYA: I'm what they call a bitch.

NEMOV: What did you say?

KOSTYA: A bitch, that's what I said, a bitch.

NEMOV: What does it mean?

KOSTYA: It means I used to be a "professional" but I gave it up. I "bitched out"—that's what they say. We get jobs as work allocators or gang bosses or head prisoners. We help the administration. The "professionals" aren't allowed to do that. Any time there are three bitches and one crook together in a room, we cut his throat. Three crooks and one bitch—they cut our throats. That's the way we get by.

NEMOV: What about me? What's the camp slang for what I am?

KOSTYA: You? I've already told you what you are, you're a mug. Little Lord Fauntleroy, that's what you are. I've no time for people like you. But you put the boot in those skivers, that's why I took a liking to you. They're thick as thieves, those skivers, they're a closed shop, like this. (*Holds up his hands with the fingers interwoven*) Mind you, I'm one of them. But there was a woman Rubyan the storekeeper and I both wanted. So either I get him sent out to cut trees, or else he gets me sent. That's why I can go along with you. We can work together. Don't worry, I'm reliable. "Mutual aid in action"—that's what they teach you in the navy. What do we do next?

NEMOV: (*By now quite drunk*) That's right, what do we do next?

KOSTYA: Kitchen: the head cook's one of my men, so that's all right. (*Crooks one finger, counting*) Bread-cutting room: we must have our own bread-cutter. That's number two. And our own quartermaster—number three . . . (*Crooks another finger*)

(*The painted curtain falls*)

(*During the interval, though not immediately after the end of the act, there is a change of sentries on the towers at the side of the stage. Having relieved one sentry, the guard party marches down into the stalls and across the auditorium in front of the first row. If members of the audience are in their way, the officer shouts at them rudely, "Get back from the wire! stop crowding!" then they relieve the other sentry*)

Act II, Scene 1

The Camp Commandant

(*The spacious office of the camp commandant. The middle of the room is empty except for a strip of red carpet. A dozen chairs in a row with their backs to the left-hand wall. Further back is a door, and behind it in the corner a large bust of Stalin on a pedestal. At the back there is a wooden-plank partition with an opening and a pair of parted curtains on either side. Through it a bed can be seen. On the right are two windows which provide the only light in the room. Outside the weather is overcast. Also on the right is a writing desk, and on it a tall inkstand in the form of a Kremlin tower. There are also some shelves with a radio set on them, and a sofa.*

It is quiet. The sound of rain falling into the drainpipes can be heard quite distinctly.

From behind the partition comes a heavy groaning noise, after which a pair of boots are lowered from the bed on to the floor. Lieutenant OVCHUKHOV *comes out into the room carrying his officer's tunic and wanders about*)

OVCHUKHOV: Blast the damn thing, where the hell is it? Bloody nuisance! God knows why they issue the things. We're not in the front line, are we? I haven't cleaned it for three years . . . If I report it I'm sunk, if I don't I'm sunk even deeper. (*Comes up to the window*) It's been pouring for nearly three days now. (*Walks up to the desk. Without sitting down he rummages around in the papers*) Look at this letter! I've only been back a few hours and it's here already. Do they drop it out of an aeroplane or something? I suppose they've got so many typists in Head

Office now, they've got to justify their wages. (*He switches on the table lamp and tears open an envelope*) Listen to this: Decision passed by full staff conference . . . Point 34: "To warn Comrade Lieutenant Ovchukhov that unless he achieves a sharp rise in productivity he will be transferred to a labour camp in the remote north of the country." They want to exile me, somewhere up in Kolyma. They're tightening the screws, they really are. (*He sits down at the desk*) There's only one way out. I'll have to report it. I'll tell them I've lost my revolver. All right, let them throw me out of the Service. I can find myself a job, can't I? Only not one with thousands of roubles a month and food from the camp store. No, I don't think so . . . Or they might put me on trial. No, they won't throw me out. They'll pull me in, blow me up sky-high, but they won't throw me out. (*Rings the bell.* ANGEL *appears in the doorway*)

ANGEL: Welcome home, citizen commandant. Would you care to order your breakfast?

OVCHUKHOV: Yes, go and get it. And send for that . . . that production chief, what's his name?

ANGEL: He's out on the site, sir.

OVCHUKHOV: Well, go and get him.

ANGEL: Yes, sir. (*He leaves.* OVCHUKHOV *sits at the desk, head in hands. A knock at the door*)

OVCHUKHOV: Come in. (*Enter* SOLOMON. *He is very neatly dressed*)

SOLOMON: May I come in? Good morning, citizen commandant. Welcome home! (OVCHUKHOV *mumbles something in reply*) Citizen commandant, this is for your breakfast. (*Puts a bottle of vodka on the desk under the lamp*)

OVCHUKHOV: Solomon, where *do* you get these things from?

SOLOMON: We do our little best, sir.

OVCHUKHOV: (*Pointing to behind the partition*) There's a glass over there, pour me one. (SOLOMON *goes behind the partition*) Turn on the light.

(*A bright light is switched on. A knock at the door. Enter the head cook dressed in white carrying a tray covered with a muslin cloth. He closes the door skilfully behind him with his foot*)

COOK: (*Putting tray down on desk*) Welcome home, sir.

OVCHUKHOV: To hell with you all, is this a conspiracy or what? Don't you know any other words?

COOK: (*Lifting the cloth*) It's *boeuf strogan*, sir.

OVCHUKHOV: (*Points*) And what's that?

COOK: Rice rissoles. *Sauce de plume.*

OVCHUKHOV: *Plume?* That sounds good. You're a good cook, aren't you? If you weren't I'd have had you on general duties long ago.

COOK: (*Indignantly*) Sir! What for?

OVCHUKHOV: (*Slyly*) You know what for. Now scram. (*Cook leaves.* SOLOMON *creeps up and presents the commandant with the glass. He drinks and starts to eat his breakfast*) Hmm, good meat this. Not from the general kitchen, I hope? Trouble is, we feed you prisoners too well. What's the meat quota these days?

SOLOMON: Half-ounce basic ration. But if it's third-category offal—gullet, say, or lungs or oxtail—then they get more. Or sometimes we substitute fish or peas.

OVCHUKHOV: It's very good meat indeed! Go on, pour me another. (SOLOMON *presents him with another glass*) Well, what's new? Let's have your report. This new production chief, how's he managing? What are you grinning about?

SOLOMON: Well, sir, you chose him, you appointed him, he must be all right.

OVCHUKHOV: Of course. I appointed him, which means he's all right. I understand about people. (*Pause*) What are you getting at?

SOLOMON: Sir, he behaves like some king, like God Almighty. Like your deputy!

OVCHUKHOV: He's quite right. That's what I told him to be when I left him in my place.

SOLOMON: I couldn't agree with you more, sir. But being in your place doesn't mean he has to go against your wishes and countermand your orders . . .

OVCHUKHOV: What's that?

SOLOMON: For instance, the other day he re-distributed the extra rations. Then he really let himself go. He put the dentist on general duties. He's been tightening up on camp personnel . . .

OVCHUKHOV: Camp personnel needs more than tightening up. I'd like to send them *all* on general duties. I've had enough of our production figures dropping. All right, you're the clerk, you can stay; the cook too, he can stay. But as for all these quarter-masters and barbers and deputy head prisoners, they can get out and do a day's work. I'm not getting posted to the North Pole on *your* account.

SOLOMON: Citizen director, you only have to say the word. If you say, "Solomon, during the day you will work in your office, during the night you will dig holes in the ground," I'll go straight out and get my pick-axe. But that Nemov—I'm not so sure about him. Another thing: the new boots—he just gave them out to anyone he felt like. He didn't get your permission.

OVCHUKHOV: He shouldn't have done that.

SOLOMON: I told him to wait till you got back, but no, he wouldn't. He's taken bribes from the new prisoners over who to send out on tree-felling.

OVCHUKHOV: Takes hands-outs, does he? Good for him. He'd be a fool if he didn't.

SOLOMON: Well, yes, I agree. But quite frankly, sir, he's not the sort of man we need here to raise our productivity. There's one man in the new transport, an engineer, talented, keen as mustard. Now he *knows* about productivity . . .

OVCHUKHOV: What does "talented" mean, I'd like to know? What is he, an opera singer? (*Reaction*) I'll deal with your men of talent, Solomon . . . (*Knock on door*) Come in!

(*Enter* NEMOV. *His clothes are all wet*)

NEMOV: Citizen director! Production chief Nemov reporting as per instructions, sir!

OVCHUKHOV: You can see he's been in the army, can't you? Well, Solomon, what about your complaints? Where's he gone wrong?

SOLOMON: I've no complaints, sir.

OVCHUKHOV: Well, if you've no complaints you can go. (*Exit* SOLOMON) And what have *you* been up to while I've been away? Bossing everyone around?

NEMOV: (*Speaking as if he was making a report to his superior officer*) Sir, I have acted strictly according to your instructions: productivity to be raised by all available means.

OVCHUKHOV: How much has it gone up, then?

NEMOV: During the past ten days productivity has been increased by eight per cent, sir.

OVCHUKHOV: That's magnificent! How did you manage it?

NEMOV: In the first place by investigating the quota office. I discovered the works department are swindling us. Sometimes they write an incomplete description of the assigned work. Sometimes they falsify the quotas.

OVCHUKHOV: Why wasn't Dorofeyev keeping his eye open for that? The bald son of a bitch! I'll send him on general duties. He's our man, from our camp. He ought to stand up for *us*, not the works department.

NEMOV: Citizen director, Dorofeyev's the one person who can't do a thing. He works for Gurvich. It won't help us if Gurvich throws him out after one day protecting our interests.

OVCHUKHOV: You know, I always felt the works department were screwing us. How much did you say you've upped production?

NEMOV: Eight per cent.

OVCHUKHOV: That's not enough, not nearly enough. It needs upping by *fifty*-eight per cent! No, not fifty-eight, sixty! Fifty-eight's something else. I'll have to see you get a few lessons, you haven't got the experience, you don't know your onions yet. (*Very distinctly*) The prisoners have to be made to *work*! Today, for instance, it's raining. Have you been out and checked? I bet none of the outside workers are doing a stroke. You must go and drive them out. They aren't putting their *souls* into the work, that's the trouble. These prisoners are lazy bastards, they'd rather give up their bread ration and starve than get off their backs. It's your job to get them by the scruff of the neck. And if you have to clip them one round the ear in the process, that's fine by me. (NEMOV *says nothiug*) Now look at this. (*He picks up a piece of paper off the table and throws it at* NEMOV) Here you are bellyaching to Gurvich about safety regulations. It's a lot of crap, and none of your business. Now, have you collected anything nice off the new transport?

NEMOV: I don't understand.

OVCHUKHOV: I mean jumpers, leather coats, silk skirts . . . Or do you want to pinch the lot for yourself?

NEMOV: I don't understand. (*Pause*) Why should I take other people's belongings?

OVCHUKHOV: To *live*, you idiot! Rule number one in the camps! "You drop dead today, I'll drop dead tomorrow"— haven't you heard that? When you fought in the war you took booty, didn't you?

NEMOV: (*Embarrassed*) Yes, I did . . .

OVCHUKHOV: It's the same thing, Little Lord Fauntleroy . . . I'm sorry, Nemov, I'm not trying to insult you, but you'll never survive in the camps this way. You won't. You know what you should have done just now? Brought me something useful. "Here's a new skirt for your wife" or something, you should have said. And I'd have loved you for it.

NEMOV: (*Very depressed*) Sir, when we first met I told you I'd been an officer in the front line, that I had experience of leadership and that I would try to sort out our production. I didn't promise anything else.

OVCHUKHOV: All right, you raise productivity by sixty per cent and I'll love you all the same. You step on the gas and I'll back you up.

NEMOV: Very well, sir. I should like to suggest that we halve the administrative personnel, get rid of those hangers-on. There are too many people wandering about inside the camp while others are outside working—for example, in the book-keeping office and in the kitchen. We seem to have two bread-cutters, three bath orderlies, even though the bath-house never seems to be working, and a million other people. There's the dentist, and I know for a fact he hasn't crowned one single tooth. And there are all those nurses in the hospital . . .

(*Knock on the door. Enter* MERESHCHUN *without waiting for an answer. He is fresh-looking, clean-shaven and thick-set. Under his white coat we can see he is wearing* KHOMICH's *bright red sweater*)

MERESHCHUN: Good morning, citizen commandant. (*He walks across the room and sits down at* OVCHUKHOV's *desk.* NEMOV *remains standing throughout*)

OVCHUKHOV: Hullo, doctor. Production chief here's been telling me you've got too many nurses. He says we ought to cut down.

MERESHCHUN: He needn't be jealous. All he has to do is to come and tell me who he wants. Manya? Clara? Certainly, take your pick! (OVCHUKHOV *roars with laughter*) I've got two nurses on my staff, one for day-duty, one for night-duty. I've got six others, but they come under "patients", they're not mine. Production chief ought to realise that.

NEMOV: In other words every day six people who are ill have to go out to work instead of going into sick-bay? I suppose this is to justify your nurses?

OVCHUKHOV: (*Waves him away*) You watch your tongue, Nemov. So what if a few extra people go out to work, the State doesn't lose anything, does it? (*To* MERESHCHUN) But it doesn't mean I don't love him, so long as he raises productivity. (*To* NEMOV) O.K., off you go. Step on it and tighten the screws! I'll back you up. (NEMOV *does a smart about-turn and leaves*) That's a very nice red sweater you're wearing . . .

MERESHCHUN: Just a minute! You're the one who owes *me* a favour, not the other way round. (*Pause*) I believe you've lost something!

OVCHUKHOV: (*Startled*) What have I lost?

MERESHCHUN: You're sure you haven't lost anything?

OVCHUKHOV: You've found it? (MERESHCHUN *takes a small packet out of his pocket.* OVCHUKHOV *quickly unwraps it, finds the gun, waves it over his head and embraces* MERESHCHUN *impulsively*)
You've done it, you wonderful man! You've saved my life! Where was it?

MERESHCHUN: (*Relishing the situation*) Do you remember, before your trip to Head Office? You came from the guardroom and called on me in my hut.

OVCHUKHOV: That's right.

MERESHCHUN: And you had a drink . . .

OVCHUKHOV: A large drink.

MERESHCHUN: And then you fell asleep . . .

OVCHUKHOV: That's what happened.

MERESHCHUN: When did you get up, in the morning? I didn't hear you, I slept through it. Then I went over to your bed and on it was lying . . .

OVCHUKHOV: Must have fallen out of the holster. Little darling! (*Fondles the gun*)

MERESHCHUN: I rushed to your study, then I rushed to the guardroom. They said you'd gone.

OVCHUKHOV: I searched high and low. I searched the ground all the way back.

MERESHCHUN: I was terrified. There's always a search before October Revolution Day. I couldn't keep it in the hut, so I wrapped it in a bit of cloth and hid it under the steps. So here we are!

OVCHUKHOV: That's superb. Thank you, Mereshchun. I was scared they'd throw me out of Security. I'd decided not to own up till next pay-day. Well, what do you want? Half my kingdom is yours! Only there's nothing you need, is there? You live better here than you would outside. You turn your nose up at the cookhouse rations, you've got as many women as you want, and as for vodka, *you're* the one who brings it to *me*. So what's it to be? You want to go into town for a week without escort? Now there's an offer! You're an Article 58 man, you know what that means?

MERESHCHUN: A trip to town? Now that's a possibility.

OVCHUKHOV: It's not a possibility at all, it's absolutely impossible. But I'll do it! I know you'll be back, you won't find a better paradise than here. What else do you want?

MERESHCHUN: Thank you, sir, I don't think there's anything else. Except perhaps . . . I'd like to help you . . .

OVCHUKHOV: Go on, go on . . .

MERESHCHUN: Why was it they called you to Head Office? They're leaning on you to achieve higher productivity? (*Pause*) Aren't they?

OVCHUKHOV: It's not a matter of leaning on me, they're squeezing hell out of me. I can hear my bones crack! They said, "We shall be forced to send you to the Arctic Circle." I've got a flat here and a family, I've started building a house . . . Well, at least the gun's been found.

MERESHCHUN: Listen, if you want to increase productivity, I've found just the man. He's perfect. He'd send his own father out into the forest if it would help his production figures.

OVCHUKHOV: Is that so? He sounds ideal. Where did you find him?

MERESHCHUN: (*Rings the little bell.* ANGEL *runs in*) Go and get engineer Khomich. He's staying in camp today, he's off sick. (ANGEL *runs out*) He's efficient, he's demanding, and he knows productivity inside out. He'll fix it for you just like that.

OVCHUKHOV: Hmm ... It would mean I'd have to sack this one.

MERESHCHUN: Which one? The Marshal? The "professionals" call him "The Marshal".

OVCHUKHOV: (*Laughs*) That's good . . .

MERESHCHUN: I was an officer myself, I can see he's the sort of man who might be used *in the army*. But he's no good here. You have to understand the *soul* of a prisoner in the camps. Five hundred grammes of black bread a day—they built the White Sea Canal on that. (*Knock at door*)

OVCHUKHOV: The soul . . . Yes, you're right. Come in. (*Enter* KHOMICH)

KHOMICH: Engineer Khomich reporting, sir.

OVCHUKHOV: What sort of engineer? Civil engineer?

KHOMICH: Yes, sir.

OVCHUKHOV: What about mechanics!

KHOMICH: I'm an engineer of that too.

OVCHUKHOV: Electrical work?

KHOMICH: I spent three years on it.

OVCHUKHOV: Sanitary installation?

KHOMICH: Yes, I know a bit about that.

OVCHUKHOV: Good heavens, the man's a miracle.

MERESHCHUN: There's one speciality he hasn't told you about—he's an engineer in human souls.

OVCHUKHOV: Is he now? Well, we'll check that right away. Suppose I make you production chief and say to you, "Increase productivity!" Where would you start?

KHOMICH: I'd start with the bread. For example, I'd issue the minimum bread guarantee for one hundred and one per cent norm fulfilment, not for one hundred as it is now. Then all those who work by the hour would switch over to piece work. It would work out in our favour. Next, I'd lower the scale for those who qualify for top rations . . .

OVCHUKHOV: Just a minute. That scale's been laid down by Camp Central Office. We can't . . .

KHOMICH: We can! Don't worry, no one's going to get into trouble. I used that dodge in my last camp. I was work superintendent. Brilliant results!

OVCHUKHOV: It's certainly a stroke of imagination.

KHOMICH: Next, we must change the scale for the porridge issues. We must make them over-fulfil their quota more and more to get an extra bowl of porridge.

OVCHUKHOV: We thought that one out ourselves. We've upped the quotas as much as we dared. If we go any higher we'll drive them over the limit. They'll turn "goner" on us.

MERESHCHUN: No, they won't. As a doctor I'm telling you they will not turn "goner".

KHOMICH: Thirdly, meetings between men and women will be

allowed only for one hundred and fifty per cent norm fulfilment. Night meetings: two hundred and one per cent qualifies for one night together, two hundred and fifty per cent for two nights. Fourthly, food parcels for prisoners who fulfil their quota by less than one hundred and twenty per cent will not be accepted from the post office.

OVCHUKHOV: Do we have the right to do that?

KHOMICH: Listen, by the time the relatives have worked things out, written complaints and sent them to Moscow, and Moscow sends them on to us, we'll have had three months to get a grip on the prisoners who live off their own food, the ones who don't need the cookhouse food. They'll realise: either work like an ox or drop dead. A very important lesson! Number five—fixing the rates. I'll manage that myself. Number six . . .

OVCHUKHOV: This is excellent stuff. How many more points?

KHOMICH: About fifteen.

OVCHUKHOV: All right, what's the sixteenth?

KHOMICH: Number sixteen—thanks to a general increase in productivity we shall be able to detail a construction team to work on your own house and finish it by the anniversary of the October Revolution!

OVCHUKHOV: That's right. That's the answer I wanted! There's carpentry to be done and painting and . . .

KHOMICH: I know, I know.

MERESHCHUN: Sixteen points altogether.

OVCHUKHOV: That's what I call efficiency—and experience. (*Rings the bell. Enter* SOLOMON, *hands behind his back*) How did you guess it was you I was ringing for?

SOLOMON: Angel had to go out for a minute, sir. I came in so that you wouldn't be kept waiting.

OVCHUKHOV: Go and get me the order book.

SOLOMON: (*Producing the book from behind his back*) Right here, sir.

OVCHUKHOV: (*Quite amazed*) You're as wise as old King Solomon! How did you guess I wanted the order book?

SOLOMON: It's my job to guess your thoughts, sir.

OVCHUKHOV: Marvellous staff I've got, marvellous! I know how to choose the right people, that's what it is. Comrade Stalin was quite right. He said, "Personnel selection is decisive. People are our most valuable capital." I want that slogan up in the camp yard!

SOLOMON: It's hanging in the canteen, sir.

OVCHUKHOV: They're a lot of fools in the culture office. All they know about is pinching wood from the construction site. I meant to tell them, "He who does not work does not eat" should be hung in the canteen. "Valuable capital" should be hung outside.

SOLOMON: I'll tell them, sir.

OVCHUKHOV: Sit down and write what I say. (SOLOMON *sits down and puts on his glasses*) Order number . . . What's the number?

SOLOMON: Two hundred and thirty six.

OVCHUKHOV: Right. Paragraph one. Prisoner . . . What's his name . . ?

MERESHCHUN: Nemov . . .

OVCHUKHOV: Prisoner Nemov, for his failure to guarantee a sharp increase in productivity, is to be dismissed from his post as . . .

SOLOMON: May I suggest, sir? It might look better if we put "for permitting a decrease in productivity"?

OVCHUKHOV: Fine, go ahead. "For permitting a decrease in productivity . . ."

MERESHCHUN: Hadn't we better say "for permitting a sharp decrease in productivity . . ."?

OVCHUKHOV: . . . is hereby dismissed for permitting a sharp decrease in productivity and output. Paragraph two. In his place I hereby appoint to the post of production chief prisoner . . .

MERESHCHUN: Prisoner Engineer Khomich!

(*Painted curtain falls*)

Act II, Scene 2

The Rate-fixing Office

(*A spacious high-ceilinged room, crudely plastered, in a building which is still under construction. By the left-hand wall is a huge awkward looking table. Further along the same wall there is a door with a plate on it reading "*SENIOR WORK SUPERINTENDENT*". In the back wall there is a door leading into the kitchen where* LYUBA *is cooking, and another door leading on to the staircase. The right-hand wall has two windows.* DOROFEYEV, *with a towel wrapped round his bald head and forehead, is sitting at the table surrounded by handbooks and papers. In the middle and towards the front of the stage there is another table belonging to no one in particular. A few roughly planned benches and stools, some broken, some in one piece.*

It is the day when percentages are calculated to determine the fulfilment of norms. The office is buzzing with various foremen filling in work order-forms, and gang bosses arguing with them. Their clothes and footwear show that it is raining and muddy. People come in and go out, writing things down either standing up or sitting down wherever they can find a place. They keep grabbing forms from the rate-fixer and spoiling them, pestering the exhausted DOROFEYEV *and taking books from the table.* NEMOV *too takes a lively part in the discussions.*

The room is dark, untidy, full of cigarette smoke and stuffy. Amid the hubbub various remarks can be heard)

GAI: What about the mortar preparation?

FOMIN: It's included in the bricklaying rate. You don't do it by hand, do you? You do it with a mixer.

CHMUTA: (*Shouting at* FOMIN) It's a double-cross on good, honest folk, do you hear? What the hell use is your mixer when it works one hour and then the current fails for the whole day? (KHOMICH *comes out of the work superintendent's room. He walks slowly across to the table at the front and sits down on it, his back to the audience*)

1st FOREMAN: These figures aren't written with a pen, they're piled up with a shovel. You can't do a hundred and twenty per cent, it'd kill you, you'd be down crawling on all fours.

1st GANG LEADER: What do you mean, only eighteen kopecks a hole? This is marking and boring, I have to use a vertical milling machine.

DOROFEYEV: My dear boy, these are norms, it's the standard rate approved by the State. It doesn't say anything about the machine you use.

2nd GANG LEADER: Plan? It's a load of shit! "Put up floor supports," they say, so I do that. "Do the flooring," they say, so I do the flooring. Now you want me to rip it up? Is it my fault if you want a cement floor? Look, production chief, if I'm not paid for this work I'll tell the gang to down tools. You'll have to appoint a dispute commission.

NEMOV: We're not responsible for your bosses' mistakes, foreman; pay for them yourself.

DOROFEYEV: Who took my handbook on concrete? Come on, who's got it? I can't work in conditions like . . .

MACHINE-SHOP FOREMAN: (*Who looks like a typical Young Communist*) What did you say? Lathe turning? Sixteen man-days? It's like something out of a comic magazine. I ask you . . .

1st GANG LEADER: It was that day when there was no electricity. The bushes were urgent, so you made us turn the lathes by hand, didn't you? You didn't talk about comic magazines then.

MACHINE-SHOP FOREMAN: Well, you'll have to phrase it differently, do you understand? You can't leave nonsense like that in a historical record . . . (*He picks up the work order-forms and takes them into the work superintendent's room*)

NEMOV: Yes or no? Are you going to pay for the floor supports, for removing them, and for two journeys carrying the boards? 1st FOREMAN: Where do you expect me to find the money? (*Enter* BRYLOV. *He saunters over and mixes with the others and then sits down next to* DOROFEYEV, *where he stays until he leaves the stage*)

GAI: What about carrying the stuff to the mixer? Why isn't that in?

DOROFEYEV: It's less than ten metres. We don't pay anything for that.

GAI: All right, it's eight metres, but it means two men all day on the barrow.

DOROFEYEV: There's nothing about it in the standard rates. Let me get on with my work.

CHMUTA: Give me that order! Give it back! (*He snatches the order-form out of the foreman's hands and tears it to pieces*) You can go and jump in the lake! The plaster falls off, so who has to do the work all over again? Me? We built the stove and you've got to pay for it . . .

GAI: Comrade Fomin, I appeal to your conscience. The men are being pushed over the limit. All day long on the barrows, then back to camp, swallow down a mug of hot water with cabbage in it and it's time to go to bed. If we could only give them some porridge in the evening.

FOMIN: I understand exactly, my dear boy. I'm exhausted myself. Look, my nose and my beard, they're all I have left in the world. They've told us to cut the orders, not to give the camp any money. I'd get the sack if I signed these puffed-up figures of yours . . .

A VOICE: That's a fine job you've done with the concrete; all the fittings have fallen out.

DOROFEYEV: Don't touch those books, don't touch them!

1st FOREMAN: (*To* DOROFEYEV) Why did you let the gang leaders get their hands on these registers? Twenty was marked down here, and now someone's added a nought—two hundred!

3rd GANG LEADER: It looks like your handwriting.

DOROFEYEV: How can I stop them? They take the damn things themselves. This place is impossible to work in.

2nd GANG LEADER: Did I put floor supports in, or did I not?

1st FOREMAN: There's something been changed here too. And here.

YAKHIMCHUK: The smiths haven't been earning a penny on these figures, not even as they stand now.

SMITH FOREMAN: How much did you earn for the chains, then? Three norms a day, wasn't it?

CHMUTA: (*Shouting*) You can't even do your job properly!

NEMOV: So you are not going to pay?

2nd FOREMAN: That's right.

NEMOV: (*To* 2nd GANG LEADER) O.K., tell your men, down tools! It's time this was put a stop to—treating everyone like slaves.

(2nd GANG LEADER *moves towards the exit but he is stopped at the door by* KHOMICH *shouting in a voice of command*)

KHOMICH: (*Sitting on the table, motionless, with his back to the audience*) Just a minute! You, gang leader, where are you off to?

2nd GANG LEADER: To tell my men to down tools. What's it to do with you?

KHOMICH: Now calm down. What's all this, a sit-down strike? Who gave you permission?

2nd GANG LEADER: Production chief gave me permission. Who do you think you are?

KHOMICH: What production chief? I'm production chief.

(*Suddenly the noise stops and is replaced by complete silence and general immobility.* LYUBA *peers out from the kitchen wearing a white apron. She freezes in this pose*)

NEMOV: You mean . . . What do you mean?

KHOMICH: I mean what I say.

NEMOV: Excuse me but . . . who appointed you?

KHOMICH: The camp commandant.

NEMOV: But I was with him half an hour ago.

KHOMICH: I was with him ten minutes ago.

NEMOV: How could it happen? He never called me in, he never told me . . .

CHMUTA: It can happen! My dear Nemov, in the camps anything can happen.

NEMOV: But why? . . . People don't behave like that . . . Not even cannibals behave like that . . . I'll go and enquire . . . No one's told me anything . . .

KHOMICH: They won't let you past the check-point. You can join your gang and work with them for the rest of the day, do your bit for the quota. (*Raising his voice*) Attention all gang leaders! I've had enough of this permanent racket over the rate-fixing. In future everyone entering this office without my permission will wish he'd never been born.

CHMUTA: Three cabinet ministers spent ten years trying to re-educate me. They got nowhere, and neither will you.

KHOMICH: (*Speaking in the same tone as before*) It's like a circus! Everyone yelling, going on strike, prisoners lounging around indoors hiding from the rain . . . Go and get them out to work, every single man!

(*The gang leaders silently and unhurriedly begin to disperse*)

DOROFEYEV: Hmm, it's so quiet all of a sudden. (*Peering at* KHOMICH *out of the corner of his eyes*) Now we'll be able to get some work done. There's going to be law and order, I can see that right away (*To* BRYLOV) I've been having such terrible headaches . . .

BRYLOV: So have I, my head's like a football.

DOROFEYEV: (*Pointedly*) *My* head aches because I'm ill.

BRYLOV: I had this dream, you see, I can't get over it, and it was days ago . . .

YAKHIMCHUK: (*To* NEMOV) What about it, then? You'll join us in the foundry?

BRYLOV: What do you think you're playing at? I'm boss in the foundry. We've got enough mouths to feed. We're short of coke. What are we going to live on?

YAKHIMCHUK: (*To* BRYLOV) Don't make so much noise. Who feeds who, that's what I want to know.

NEMOV: I'm very grateful to you comrade, but it depends on whether . . . (*Looks at* KHOMICH)

KHOMICH: You see, I'm a gentleman. You never did *me* any harm personally. If Yakhimchuk wants you, that's all right by me.

BRYLOV: What do you mean "all right by you"? I don't want him, I'm boss in the foundry!

(YAKHIMCHUK *leads* NEMOV *away. Now that the gang leaders have left, the foremen begin to leave as well.* KHOMICH *jumps off the table and comes right to the front of the stage*)

KHOMICH: Dorofeyev . . .(DOROFEYEV *stands up hurriedly*)

DOROFEYEV: Yes, sir, I'm listening. (*He walks up to him*)

KHOMICH: (*So that the others can't hear him*) The camp commandant has assigned you a task. It is your job to *double* the productivity of every single gang!

DOROFEYEV: S-sir, how can I do that? If it says one rouble in the book how can I make it two roubles?

KHOMICH: Stop trying to find someone stupider than yourself, Dorofeyev, and stop swinging the lead. All right, it's thirty-two kopecks for a metre of plaster work, everyone knows that. But what about, say, a conic pinion? How long does it take to make one of those? Ten hours? Fifty hours? Who the hell knows?

DOROFEYEV: But that's a criminal offence. I don't want to get a second term. They're standard rates which the State has . . .

KHOMICH: What State? This isn't a State, this is Campland!

DOROFEYEV: Gurvich'll find out in no time. He'll give me the sack.

KHOMICH: If he does we'll fix you up inside the camp. We'll keep you warm. But if *we* kick you out, you'll drop dead under a tree. Do you understand? (*Enter* ZINA *from the right. She is all dolled up, carrying a sheaf of papers and walking towards* GURVICH's *office*)

ZINA: Congratulations! (*She shakes* KHOMICH's *hand*) I heard about it yesterday.

KHOMICH: (*Walking away from* DOROFEYEV) You couldn't have heard yesterday. I was only appointed today.

ZINA: My old man Pososhkov knew about it yesterday. He finds everything out, knows it all before the commandant does. Tonight we're having a party in your honour. You haven't got a wife yet, have you? You'd better get moving.

KHOMICH: Ah-hh, the sweet life . . . "My lovely, silly happiness with white windows looking out on to the orchard... "(*Exit right.* GURVICH, *a pack of work order-forms in his hand, comes smartly out of his room and runs into* ZINA. *The machine-shop foreman is with him*)

GURVICH: Dorofeyev? (DOROFEYEV *jumps up*) These metalworkers' figures—you cooked them, didn't you? (*He throws the order-forms at* DOROFEYEV *across the room.* DOROFEYEV *picks them up hurriedly*) How much did you rate them per washer?

DOROFEYEV: Three kopecks, comrade Gurvich. Just like it says in the handbook . . .

GURVICH: Do you realise there are four thousand washers? You know how much they'll collect that way? Change it to three-tenths of a kopeck.

DOROFEYEV: But comrade Gurvich, they're standard State-approved rates . . .

GURVICH: That's enough about the State. Any more of this talk and I'll sling you out and have you laying bricks. I'll replace you with a non-prisoner. You and the camp boys are thick as thieves, aren't you? You've got gang leaders on your back the whole time, making you fix the order-forms. You'd better watch it, people end up in court for what you're doing. (*He flips through a document which* ZINA *has just handed him*) Just a minute . . . "Prisoner Matveyev fell down the shaft because there was no proper fence round the . . ." What's this nonsense? Take it away and type it out again. Write: "In spite of the adequate fencing round the shaft, Prisoner Matveyev flung himself over the edge with the intention of committing . . ."

ZINA: But the safety inspector will . . .

GURVICH: He's not an inspector, he's a bloody fool, he'll agree to anything we say. Don't worry, I've fixed it. Do it out in four copies . . . (*Moves* ZINA *to one side. She leaves*) Brylov, what about this bronze?

BRYLOV: Don't worry, it's in the bag. I know about these furnaces, I'll tell Munitsa how to do it. We'll get you the best bronze.

GURVICH: Yes, but when?

BRYLOV: Three days' time.

GURVICH: That's no good, I want it tomorrow. First smelting tomorrow.

LYUBA: (*Barring his way*) Dinner's ready, comrade Gurvich.

GURVICH: I haven't got time for dinner . . .

LYUBA: It'll dry up and boil away. What do we do, then?
(GURVICH *waves his hands and leaves, accompanied by the machine-shop foreman*)

BRYLOV: "First smelting tomorrow"—huh! Quick as a flea, isn't he? I'll complain about him to Head Office. "High-quality iron," he says. How the hell? One—there's no ambulatory, two—we have to charge the furnace by eye, three—the coating isn't right, four—there's no manganese. Shall I complain?

(DOROFEYEV *sits there in silence, head in hands.* KOLODEY *walks in slowly and looks around*)

KOLODEY: Well, how are things? Everything in order? No rules being broken? (*Silence*) Dorofeyev, what do you use for sharpening pencils?

DOROFEYEV: A razor-blade, citizen commander. We've got a little bit of razor-blade.

KOLODEY: Don't you know cutting and stabbing objects are against the rules?

LYUBA: How can I peel Gurvich's potatoes, then?

KOLODEY: Use your teeth for all I care. But no knives! Have you got any knives in the kitchen?

LYUBA: No.

KOLODEY: I should think not. (*Sits down and lights a cigarette*) All right, Lyuba, which girl in your barrack-room keeps sneaking off and spending every night in the men's quarters?

LYUBA: How should I know? I sleep during the night.

KOLODEY: I know, you lot are always asleep. Then I lift up the blanket and find it's a dummy, or else there's a man in with you. Then two seconds later you're dragged off to hospital to produce some squalling brat. Who does your work while you're in hospital?

LYUBA: I don't see how you can ban love-making. We're not made of wood. We're in here for ten years.

KOLODEY: If they ban it, they ban it, and that's that. You shouldn't have committed crimes, should you?

LYUBA: That's right. Just think how many children are born in the camps. They all ought to be strangled at birth.

KOLODEY: (*Startled*) What do you mean?

LYUBA: What else can we do with them? If the father's a criminal and the mother's a criminal, what sort of a child's it going to be? Another criminal. How's it going to fill in those forms when it grows up?

KOLODEY: We-ell, yes. Perhaps you're right . . .

LYUBA: But then on the other hand I'm wrong. A son's not responsible for what his father did, is he? Maybe we ought to be glad there are children born in the camps. If every woman had a child, that'd mean millions of extra soldiers, right?

KOLODEY: That's true, very true . . . (*He sighs and stands up*) Oh well, you'll do what you're told, that's one thing for sure. Poor Comrade Stalin—so many worries, so many things to think about! All right, keep working. (*Exit*)

DOROFEYEV: (*In despair to* BRYLOV) Who invented this damn rate-fixing? Before the Revolution I worked as an apprentice to a State-employed foreman. We had no rate-fixing, no book-keeping, but we built a house that'll stand for a hundred years without repair. Do you remember the way it was?

BRYLOV: No ambulatory, no scales, sub-standard coating—I'll have to complain . . . (*Exit*)

LYUBA: (*Standing stock-still by the window*) Keep working, keep working—poor wretched prisoners, rain or snow, that's all there is to do. Then back to camp, off with the wet things, dry them out—only where? In bed, that's where. Bed's the only warm place in the camp. (*To* DOROFEYEV) Is your head still aching?

DOROFEYEV: You're a sweet girl, Lyuba. If only I could take a spade and go out in the mud with the others. Anything rather than torture myself in here. They're squeezing me on both sides, I can't even breathe . . .

LYUBA: (*Sits down on the table at the front, facing the audience*) No, Dorofeyev, you're wrong. Winter's coming, we're better off here. When the snowstorms start and they make you dig solid frozen earth without even a pair of gloves . . . Oh no.

DOROFEYEV: I'll probably die soon. They say there's going to be another amnesty before Revolution Day. All the Article 58 prisoners will be released. They say it's there, lying on Stalin's desk, all he has to do is sign it . . .

LYUBA: Come off it, the only release we'll get is into the next world . . . (*Pause*) I feel sorry for him . . .

DOROFEYEV: Who?

LYUBA: Him . . . you know . . . Nemov.

DOROFEYEV: Aren't you sorry for yourself?

LYUBA: Sorry for myself? No. Not any more.

(*The painted curtain falls*)

(*During the interval the sentries on the towers are changed as before*)

Act III, Scene 1

The Bronze Has Got Stuck

(*The foundry, as in Scene Two, except that this time the moulding earth has been shaped into a cone. In various places new moulding has been started. On the left and towards the back of the stage is a furnace for smelting bronze, a round brick structure with a tin hood and a flue which disappears into the ceiling. A constant tapping sound can be heard coming from the cupola-shaped furnace on the right, underneath which a pair of feet can be seen. Near the front of the stage* MUNITSA *and* CHEGENYOV *are sitting on the floor*)

CHEGENYOV: You know what's happened? They've gone soft. Ten years? They ought to give idiots like you twenty-five! All right, I'm not going to touch it, you sort your own damn furnace out.

(MUNITSA *sits there, silent and depressed. Enter* BRYLOV. *He sits down next to them on the floor*)

BRYLOV: You know, Munitsa, you're a stupid bugger. You are, you know. Do you think it's only your Rumania that's got furnaces? You think there aren't any in mother Russia? I've forgotten more about furnaces than you've ever clapped your eyes on, *but* . . . I keep my mouth shut. You know why I keep my mouth shut? Because life's easier without furnaces. No one pesters you. So long as there's coke, there's iron. Pour it in the moulds bit by bit, enough for you, enough for us. What more can a guy ask for, eh? What more can a guy ask?

CHEGENYOV: Well, for one thing, we ask for some butter. The stuff you brought was sour.

BRYLOV: You're crazy! How can butter be sour?

CHEGENYOV: Well, it is and that's that. It's all puffy and runny like cream cheese. Still on the make, aren't you? Only you'll never get rich the way you do it.

BRYLOV: Come on, boys, what's the matter? Something wrong? Well, maybe my old woman made a mistake. Maybe she had one too many and bought the wrong kind of butter.

CHEGENYOV: She drinks too, does she?

BRYLOV: My dear boy, who doesn't drink these days? My first wife kept herself in hand, but this one's pissed half the time. Mind you, she'd have to be a saint not to. I keep a crate of vodka under our bed. It's never empty. If it was, I'd never get a wink of sleep!

MUNITSA: So what Gurvich say?

BRYLOV: I have to carry the can, that's what. It's all my fault. "Brylov mucked up the bronze." "Brylov stopped the excavators." Did I make any promises? No, I did not. I always said that furnace of yours was a washout.

MUNITSA: But bronze must be! It must be!

BRYLOV: It'll pour down and make a hole in your head . . . You'll never make the big time, Munitsa. There are plenty of people cleverer than you in the world, but no one's ever thought up a furnace like yours. If it was that simple any fool could build a furnace. Now you'd better think up a way to break it open. You've ruined forty kilos of bronze, just burnt it up. All right, to hell with the bronze, it's not our money. But it'll be a problem to break open the furnace. The bronze has got stuck.

MUNITSA: We break it quick.

(*Enter* YAKHIMCHUK *from the right*)

BRYLOV: (*To* YAKHIMCHUK) He still wants to build his damn furnace.

YAKHIMCHUK: Well, why not? So long as he does it proper.

MUNITSA: How? How I do it proper?

YAKHIMCHUK: No ideas? You were the one who wanted to.

BRYLOV: I see, you're all against me, are you? All right, I'll throw the lot of you out and get my own men. It was bad enough when you brought your damn Marshal into the place. (*Nods in the direction of the cupola*) Sponger! Why did you have to saddle me with him? The coke's running out, the iron's running out, what are we going to live on?

MUNITSA: (*Losing his temper*) This man no good. He son of a bitch, he can't do nothing!

CHEGENYOV: (*Reaches out for a spade*) You grits-eating jerk, I'll get you! You can't talk to a Don Cossack like that . . .

MUNITSA: (*To* YAKHIMCHUK) But how? How to do it?

YAKHIMCHUK: I don't know. I'm not the one going for a bonus.

MUNITSA: So, you don't know. So don't say you know.

YAKHIMCHUK: But what if I do know?

MUNITSA: What if you don't know?

BRYLOV: I wish I'd never clapped eyes on the damn thing . . .

CHEGENYOV: Don't tell him, boss. Don't tell him. He'll collect a hundred thousand roubles . . .

YAKHIMCHUK: Cabbage-head! You need a narrower burner and smaller air-ducts. Those gaping holes aren't any good. (GURVICH *walks quickly in*)

GURVICH: O.K., what's this, a boy scouts' rally? First you make a mess of the bronze and now here you are holding meetings. You're a big-head, Munitsa, aren't you?

MUNITSA: You wait. Bronze in pipeline.

GURVICH: You lot have got everything in the pipeline—frying pans, irons, cooking pots. You're supplying the town with consumer goods better than a Moscow shop. I ought to post the lot of you, have you out cutting trees . . .

BRYLOV: My boys haven't done anything wrong. The furnace is impossible. Ask the engineers. I've been in foundries since I was so high, I don't like this sort of talk. You'd better send me to the Urals to organise those crucibles . . .

GURVICH: Send you to the Urals? I'd rather send you down the river. Look at this planing machine! You've got it turning out irons non-stop, haven't you? There's no time for the machine parts. (*He comes up to* YAKHIMCHUK *and puts his hands round his shoulder*) Yakhimchuk, I appeal to you, as one human being to another, think of something, help me. The excavators are standing idle, they're not earning a penny. Can't we get a temporary furnace going, boys? Just for one smelting?

MUNITSA: O.K., Comrade Gurvich, we change burner, we change ducts, we get bronze. We get first-class bronze.

(*Enter* MACHINE-SHOP FOREMAN)

MACHINE-SHOP FOREMAN: (*To* GURVICH) Cutting press has stopped, sir.

GURVICH: (*As if bitten by a snake*) Oh no, not again! Yakhimchuk, you will help us? Munitsa, please, you'll get a bonus. Don't let me down, boys . . .

(*He and the foreman stride out*)

BRYLOV: (*To them all*) Don't do it! Just tell him you can't and that's that. I have to go now. Do what you can. If Gurvich wants to know where I am, say I'm at construction site number one . . . or number two . . . (*Exit*)

CHEGENYOV: Who's been squealing to Gurvich about the irons? They're at us for things we don't even make. These damn squealers are making life impossible . . .

(*Exit*)

YAKHIMCHUK: O.K., Munitsa, we'll go fifty-fifty on the bonus, right? (MUNITSA *does not answer*) I was only joking. I'd never have said anything, only you're ruining all our work. It hurts me to see it. You and Gurvich have gone completely off beam. Where's the pencil? Come on, I'll draw it for you . . .

MUNITSA: We do brickwork together, right?

YAKHIMCHUK: All right, fine. (*They leave on the right. The stage is empty. The tapping sound inside the cupola stops. Enter* LYUBA *from the left*)

LYUBA: Comrade Gurvich, telephone for you . . . Where is he? He must have dashed out. (*She looks into the room on the right, then comes back. Someone emerges from under the cupola*) Oy, who's that?

(*It is* NEMOV. *He straightens up. His canvas overalls are so torn that in places his skin can be seen through them. His face and his torn cap are covered with grey dust. He is wearing a pair of home-made celluloid spectacles and carrying a chisel and a hammer*)

NEMOV: It's me. Don't you recognise me?

LYUBA: No-oo, it can't be! You look a sight! (*She laughs buoyantly.* NEMOV *lifts his glasses, smiles and scratches his head with his hammer*) How did you fit in there? There's not room.

NEMOV: Yes, it *was* a bit cramped. But I'm thinner these days. If only there wasn't so much dust . . . Lyuba, that's your name, isn't it?

LYUBA: You've remembered? Such a cold, efficient production chief. You never seemed to notice who anyone was.

NEMOV: Yes, you've got something there. I was still trying to get in with the authorities. A sudden crash and there I was still trying to pull myself back at the last step. In those days I preferred to bend others than to bend myself. But I feel freer now I'm an ordinary black-faced working man.

LYUBA: There's only one thing wrong with being a black-faced worker—they die.

NEMOV: Well, look at me—chiselling off the slag, singing songs . . .

LYUBA: That's because you're in the foundry. You get good rations in the foundry.

NEMOV: You know something—sometimes I think to myself, are our lives so important? Are they the most valuable thing we have?

LYUBA: (*With great attention*) What else is there?

NEMOV: It sounds funny talking about it here in the camp, but maybe . . . conscience . . .

LYUBA: (*Gazing at him intently*) Do you think so?
(*Pause*)

NEMOV: How are your hands? I remember you had trouble with them.

LYUBA: My hands? (*She holds them out*)

NEMOV: But that's impossible! (*He drops the chisel and hammer and takes* LYUBA *by the hands*) They're so beautiful and white. It's all gone?

LYUBA: (*Laughs out loud*) There was never anything there.

NEMOV: What do you mean? I saw it with my own eyes, black blisters all round here . . .

LYUBA: I was swinging the lead!

NEMOV: What does that mean?

LYUBA: I swung the lead, so as not to go on that transport. "Swinging the lead" is what they call it in the camp when you fix it to look ill—like a tumour or a blind eye or a fever.

NEMOV: Can you really do it?

LYUBA: He doesn't believe me! 'Course I can. I fooled you, didn't I?

NEMOV: It's fantastic. How did you fool the warder?

LYUBA: Oh, I think he guessed. But he took pity on me. Wouldn't you have taken pity on me?

NEMOV: . . . Probably not . . .

LYUBA: Have you finished examining my hands? Why don't you let go of them?

NEMOV: I need them . . .

LYUBA: What for? (NEMOV *kisses* LYUBA's *hands*) You're not going to pretend you like me?

NEMOV: How can you say that?

LYUBA: When they brought us in—I mean the new transport—they made us sit on the ground. You came up to the women, you looked us all over and you chose . . . Granya. Do you remember?

NEMOV: Just a minute . . . what did you think when I chose Granya?

LYUBA: I thought, why didn't he choose me?

NEMOV: It's simple, it was a different criterion.

LYUBA: But your eyes were open, weren't they? How could you have chosen anyone else!

NEMOV: Lyuba, I was looking for a gang leader, someone with drive . . .

LYUBA: I was terribly offended.

NEMOV: Of course I noticed immediately how . . . how pretty you are.

LYUBA: So why did you try to send me out into the forests?

NEMOV: They needed a barber.

LYUBA: Why should I suffer because of that?

NEMOV: No, of course not, there's no reason why you should suffer. A girl like you should wear a fine, white dress, with lilies of the valley pinned here, across the breast. Even in that uniform quilt jacket you look . . . Give me your hands.

LYUBA: What for?

NEMOV: To kiss.

LYUBA: What sort of man kisses like that? On the hands?

NEMOV: It's all I dare.

LYUBA: You're funny. (NEMOV *kisses her hands*) Your hands are all cut.

NEMOV: The slag's sharp. I have to hammer it out with a chisel. Sometimes I miss.

LYUBA: What a life! It's hard for you, isn't it?

NEMOV: It's almost a year now since I was arrested. Since then it's been nothing but gloom and misery. Now for the first time I feel happy.

LYUBA: Happy? On general duties?

NEMOV: Now that you're here . . .

LYUBA: I was here when you were one of the bosses.

NEMOV: It's wonderful not being one of the bosses. If I was I'd think you were trying to get something out of me. But now . . .

LYUBA: Now it's time I went. Let go of me.

NEMOV: Don't go.

LYUBA: Are we just going to stand here, like this? (NEMOV *mumbles something*) Come to the culture room this evening. There's going to be a concert. Come backstage. (*She moves slowly away from him, her back to the door*)

NEMOV: (*Walking slowly after her*) Will I see you then, Lyuba? (LYUBA *nods her head and leaves.* NEMOV *stops and stands there gazing after her. The painted curtain falls*)

Act III, Scene 2

On the Roof

(This scene takes place on top of a building under construction, with the sky as a background. It is not the roof but a partition between two storeys. So far the outside wall at the back of the stage has been built up a mere half-metre above floor level. Two broad square pillars with descending staircases flank the wall, rising another metre above it. From the left-hand pillar an inside wall runs towards the audience. Two pairs of bricklayers are standing on some scaffolding laying the wall. The wall comes almost up to the curtain, and so forms a passage to the left there. A similar right-angled inside wall has been begun from the right-hand pillar but abandoned. To the right of the right-hand pillar, invisible to the audience, stands a "pioneer"-type crane. The only visible part of it is its turning carrier, which can be seen lifting a platform and carrying it over the back wall. Each time it does this the platform has two wheelbarrows on it.

Wooden planks are laid across the long beams of the flooring to form tracks for the wheelbarrows, leading up from the crane platform to the scaffolding by the left-hand wall. GRANYA *and* SHUROCHKA, *both in quilted trousers, are pushing the wheelbarrows over to the wall, turning them over to pour the mortar out for the four bricklayers, returning the wheelbarrows to the crane platform and transferring the hook from the full platform to the empty one.*

A pair of "drudge" prisoners are pushing barrows of bricks from the right over to the left-hand wall, about thirty bricks at a time. As the curtain rises GAI *is standing on a small raised platform in the right-hand corner of the stage, watching the others work, glumly and in silence. It is a warm sunny day, one of the last good days of autumn. A crane is lifting a platform with two wheelbarrows on it. A couple of professional crooks, GOLDTOOTH and GEORGIE, appear from the right pushing a barrow. They are naked to the waist, brawny and covered with tattoo-marks. They don't walk, they dance across the stage, and in their barrow there are only three bricks. They tip the bricks off on to the scaffolding and leave the stage, dancing and humming as usual, glancing from time to time at the gang leader)*

1st BRICKLAYER: (*After the two professionals have gone*) Comrade Gai, please get some more carriers, I've no bricks to lay. Are they playing games or what?

(*GAI says nothing. Meanwhile GRANYA and SHUROCHKA have wheeled their barrows over to the left-hand wall and returned to the right-hand pillar*)

SHUROCHKA: (*Hanging her head*) My God, it's hard work . . . Roll on break-time . . .

GRANYA: (*Looking into the distance*) Over there I can see a cart . . . It's got a load of straw.

SHUROCHKA: How can you see it's straw?

GRANYA: I can spot a hare at half a mile. You smell the breeze? I can smell fallen leaves, it's from the forest, far over there . . . (*She breathes air in*)

SHUROCHKA: Can you really smell the leaves? If only we could go outside, if only we could rest and forget it all . . .

GRANYA: Not me, I'm better as I am.

SHUROCHKA: How can you say that?

GRANYA: I've had my fill of air in the camps, I've seen so much meanness and ghastliness. I'd never be able to rest, not even outside.

(*The crane brings over a new platform.* GRANYA *transfers the hook and trundles the wheelbarrow noisily away to the left and off stage. There are tracks for the wheelbarrow laid there as well.* SHUROCHKA *follows her, pushing her wheelbarrow with an effort*)

2nd BRICKLAYER: (*To* 1st BRICKLAYER) I got a parcel notification. My family sent me a parcel, but the bastards here sent it back. No parcels till I up my figures to a hundred and twenty per cent, that's what they say. It's my own property too, my own food! Can they do that to me? I'll do my damnedest to see the commandant about it today.

1st BRICKLAYER: 'Course they can do it to you. They can do anything. (*Reaction*) Justice? It doesn't exist. Look at us drudges slaving away while the professionals take it easy. Do you think the gang leader will give them less rations than he gives you?

2nd BRICKLAYER: Our boss? Gai? You wait, he won't give in to them.

(4th BRICKLAYER, *an auxiliary worker who looks completely exhausted, collapses and sits down on the ground*)

3rd BRICKLAYER: Mishka! What's the matter?

4th BRICKLAYER: My head's going round and round. Let me sit for a while. I just can't . . .

2nd BRICKLAYER: Let him sit down for a few minutes . . .

3rd BRICKLAYER: What do you mean, let him sit down? Why should I do double duty?

2nd BRICKLAYER: I'll give you a hand. The boy's a "goner". And no wonder, he won't drink hot water. How can he keep his strength up?

(*They carry on working. The "drudge" prisoners push their overloaded barrow to the wall almost at the double, empty it and push it back.* GOLDTOOTH *and* GEORGIE *appear, walking as usual with their swinging dance-like gait. This time there is only one brick on their barrow. They throw* GAI *several glances as they go past him, then drop their barrow and sit down.* GRANYA *and* SHUROCHKA *carry on working*)

GEORGIE: O.K., that's the lot. Lets get some sun. (*He lies down to sun himself.* GOLDTOOTH *sits down and begins to sing a disgusting little song glorifying professional crooks. His body twitches as he sings, and he makes a face like a monkey.* GAI *remains motionless throughout the song. A wardress enters from the left, a mane of curls sticking out from under her military cap. Seeing the* 4th BRICKLAYER *resting, she creeps up to him and strikes him a blow on the neck*)

WARDRESS: Lazy son of a bitch! Get up and work! (4th BRICKLAYER *gets up with difficulty and begins to pass bricks to the* 3rd BRICKLAYER. *The other bricklayers quicken their pace of work.* GOLDTOOTH *carries on singing and grimacing. The wardress walks over to the professional crooks and addresses* GEORGIE) You, what are you showing everyone your belly for? You think it's beautiful?

GEORGIE: (*Lying there*) Hullo, darling, come over here. Lie down, we'll have a roll in the hay.

WARDRESS: Huh! Asking a bit much, aren't you? (*Exit right*)

GOLDTOOTH: All right, let's have a smoke, O.K.? Give us a bit of paper, boss. (GAI *remains quite motionless*)

FOMIN: (*He walks straight across the stage*) Hurry up, Gai! This wall's taking much too long. (*Points at the left-hand wall*) Look at it, it's holding us all up. (GAI *does not move*)

GEORGIE: (*Sits up*) Hey, boss, come over here. Let's have a smoke. We'd better have a talk—about things in general.

(*Immediately* GAI *gets off his perch, strides across the stage and sits down next to them*)

GOLDTOOTH: Look here, boss, you've got to learn the rules. The likes of us aren't supposed to work. We've only been working . . . out of respect. You'd better take our barrows and give them to someone else. Let the drudges sweat.

GEORGIE: In other words, we're "pros". Do you see?

GAI: "Professionals"?

GEORGIE: That's right.

GAI: What about rations?

GEORGIE: Oh, we get rations same as the rest. At least, we take the bread ration. We don't like the soup, you can give ours to the drudges. Most of our grub we get straight from the kitchen. We've butter and lard up to here. (*Hand under chin*)

GAI: And who does the work?

GEORGIE: You mean, who gets yoked? The peasants, they get yoked. The small fry. And the gentlemen fascists, the Article fifty-eight boys.

GAI: How can we earn a proper ration? How can I feed my men?

GOLDTOOTH: That's your headache. You'll have to settle that one with the screws.

GEORGIE: (*To* GOLDTOOTH, *indicating* GAI) He's got something there, you know. Suck your cock and you won't starve. That's the kind of camp this is. Don't be a mug, then you can eat with us, with the best people.

GAI: Well if you're "pros" and you're not allowed to work, why don't you stay in camp? Why push down the rest of the gang's productivity?

GEORGIE: You know, boss, you want to grow up . . .

GOLDTOOTH: Looking for someone stupider than yourself?

GEORGIE: We're not shirkers. Cross my heart and hope to rot in jail if we are. During the war they used to parade everyone for work. Any shirkers—they'd just bump them off.

GOLDTOOTH: We'd rather live a little longer.

GEORGIE: You die today, I'll die tomorrow.

GOLDTOOTH: You'll sort out the productivity. That's what a gang leader's for.

(GAI *gets to his feet and suddenly strikes one of the crooks full in the face, so hard that he falls over onto his back.* GAI *deals with the second crook likewise. They try to get up but* GAI *keeps pummeling them and prevents them from rising*)

GOLDTOOTH: What's the matter with him? Son of a bitch! Bitch!

GEORGIE: What are you doing? Stop it! You cheap bum! Bastard!

GAI: Who's a bastard? (*Hits him*)

GOLDTOOTH: Fascist.

GAI: Who's a fascist? (*Hits him*)

GEORGIE: (*Managing to get to one side*) Help! Fascists! The fascists are killing us!

(*Enter* GURVICH *quickly, followed by* FOMIN *and* KHOMICH. *They pretend not to notice the fighting. In his hands* GURVICH *is holding an unrolled builder's plan.* KHOMICH *is playing with a slide rule*)

GURVICH: That's right, a brick and a half thick, that's what it says. You call this a brick and a half? You must be blind. Can't you read a plan? (*Points at the left-hand wall*) Gai, I want that wall torn down. Do you hear? Tear it right down!

(*The professional crooks leave towards the right, mumbling threateningly.* FOMIN *scratches the back of his head*)

KHOMICH: Sorry, my dear sir, no can do. You'll have to give us a chit for that.

GURVICH: A chit? For tearing down a wall? A summons to court, that's more like it. Half our foremen are drunk, the other half illiterate . . .

KHOMICH: That's your business. If you want, we can call it evacuation of rubbish.

GURVICH: I'll see it comes out of his wages. (*Points at* FOMIN, *who wipes his spectacles, lowers his head and buries himself in the builder's plan*)

KHOMICH: (*Working something out on the slide rule*) . . . Manual transportation of rubbish to a distance of more than a hundred metres, involving a lift of ten metres, the total capacity in cubic metres being . . .

GURVICH: What lift? We've been through the orders for the last three years. More rubbish has been removed than the volume of the whole building . . .

KHOMICH: Then obviously the rubbish heap must be enormous. That explains why it has to be lifted ten metres.

GURVICH: I'll sign a chit for snow, for removal of snow.

KHOMICH: Snow's cheap. You'll have to sign for more than a cubic kilometre to pay us back for that wall.

GURVICH: Snow's the best thing. One day it's here, the next day it's melted. Control can't complain. All right, Gai, break down the wall. Lay it again, this time two bricks thick.

GAI: (*Gloomily, shouting towards the crane*) Zhenka, give them a shout will you? We want crowbars and large hammers. No more mortar for the moment.

(*Exit* GURVICH *followed by* KHOMICH. ZHENKA *peers out from the right wing and shouts down at the crane men, his voice rumbling like thunder*)

ZHENKA: Hey! You clowns down there! Go to the tool-shed, get two crowbars and two large hammers, and bring them back to the crane! (*He vanishes*)

FOMIN: (*To* GAI) Try and break it down so that the bricks stay in one piece, will you?

GAI: How the hell do you expect me to do that? Go on, show me! (FOMIN *waves one arm and walks away.* GAI *addresses his workers*)

Carry the bricks over here for the moment. (*He points left*) Shurochka, you go and help move the bricks.

(SHUROCHKA *leaves. The workers begin to carry the bricks over to the left.* GAI *sits down*)

GRANYA: (*To* GAI) What do I do?

GAI: Wait a second. I'll find you a job soon.

GRANYA: You're so brave taking on two men by yourself. Especially two like that.

GAI: It's the only way to handle them. Ever since I was in my first transit prison I've done my best to kick those damn "pros". They're parasites, and I'll go on kicking them till I'm in my last camp. You see we're "enemies of the people" and they're "friends of the people". I reckon the authorities keep them just to suck our blood. We politicals are given to them to torment. They don't separate us in the cells or in the transports. Everyone's terrified of them.

(*The crane brings over the crowbars and hammers. The bricklayers take them and begin hammering at the wall. It yields to the blows. Bricks, broken as well as in one piece, begin to fall out of it.* GAI *just sits there gloomily*)

GRANYA: Why do you frown all the time? Wondering how to feed the men?

GAI: It's a dog's life, being a gang leader. Why did I take it on? If some poor drudge gets too weak to fulfil his norm, what am I to do about it? Beat him up?

GRANYA: Someone's got to be gang leader. If it wasn't you it'd be someone else, and he might be a bastard. It would only make it worse for the drudges.

GAI: That's a dangerous argument... (*He is plunged into thought. A long pause. The noise of people working on a construction site*) My division ended the war on the River Elbe, and now look at me, stuck here. The deserters are all released, the men from the front-line are kept inside. What next? It's incomprehensible. But what can we do about it?

GRANYA: You don't have to answer those questions. Your brain can't deal with everything.

GAI: Who else is going to deal with it? (*He sighs*) I had some friends in my cell once. I was being questioned by counter-espionage. But now we are scattered all over the country. They sent some of us to Yenisei, some to Jezkazgan, some God knows where . . .

GRANYA: (*Takes him by the shoulders*) You have a friend here too.

GAI: You're a woman. And you're not a political.

GRANYA: I went through the war the same as you did. I stabbed a German scout to death with a bayonet. I ferried myself across the same rivers and bit the ground on the same bridgeheads.

GAI: They'll give you an amnesty. In a year you'll have forgotten the whole thing.

GRANYA: So will you.

GAI: Oh no, I won't forget. (KHOMICH *enters, but steps back as he notices them*) I'll tell you something—there was a guy in our cell who used to say that if people didn't live in families, no tyrant would be able to stay on his throne. He'd be washed away as if by a flood. And that's the way it is. They break our necks and all we do is start families.

GRANYA: What are you talking about? There aren't any families in this place.

GAI: It's the same here as everywhere else. Our hands and feet are tied by "love". There's a new fashion just started in our culture room—dancing to the accordion. So what happens? Everyone dances! Idiots! Ten years for doing damn all, and they dance!

GRANYA: Just my luck, falling for a cold fish like you. You'll feel sorry for me too one day. Yes, even you . . .

(*From somewhere down below behind the building comes the sound of a rail being banged by an iron bar. The bricklayers stop work abruptly. Enter* ZHENKA *from the right*)

ZHENKA: O.K., take it easy! Our gang's last for dinner (*He lies down*)

2nd BRICKLAYER: He's right, boys, let's take a nap. All that rummaging during the night, we're short on sleep.

(*The bricklayers find places for themselves and lie down on the scaffolding.* GAI *goes to the middle of the stage, lies down on his back and stays quite motionless.* SHUROCHKA *sits down where* GAI *had been sitting, next to* GRANYA. *She looks at herself in a pocket mirror*)

SHUROCHKA: The years are passing, Granya . . . I think we ought to get married while we're here in the camp. Who'll want us later on when we're outside? (*Pause*) Is it true what they are saying? That Khomich offered to put you in charge of the bread-cutting room, and you refused?

GRANYA: He did.

SHUROCHKA: I don't believe it! You're turning into some kind of wishy-washy intellectual. Turn down the bread-cutting room? I've never heard of such a thing. Plenty to eat, warm in winter, skirt and blouse, not these damn quilted trousers all leaking at the seams, no need to sweat your guts out . . .

GRANYA: What sort of a person cheats a drudge out of his bread ration even by a gramme? I made my decision—I'm not going to live like other people do in the camps. There's only one important thing—I won't see myself turned into a bastard. Live or die —what's the difference?

(KHOMICH *appears again and walks across the front of the stage*)

KHOMICH: Hello, Granya (*Pause.* GRANYA *gets up and goes to meet him*) Listen to me, my lady, there's something I want to get straight: you and Mr Gai are like that, aren't you? (*Lays one finger across the other*)

GRANYA: (*Something occurs to her*) You're not planning to have him posted?

KHOMICH: What do you mean? It's not my decision. (*He tries to walk on, but she stops him*)

GRANYA: There is something I'm longing to ask you . . . You get extra pay . . . working for the security department, don't you?

KHOMICH: (*Flinching*) How dare you! Let me go!

GRANYA: (*Holds him back*) You're preparing a file on him? You're out to get him, is that right? (*She gives him a shake*) I'll tell you one thing: if they get him on some security rap, or if they send him on a transport . . . I'll kill you!

KHOMICH: You're out of your mind! What's it got to do with me?

GRANYA: Just watch it. I don't waste words. I killed a man once, he was worth a dozen of you. Killing you would be like squeezing a caterpillar, a green caterpillar . . . (*She pushes him away*)

KHOMICH: You . . . You must be some kind of a witch. I've never met a woman like you before. You've no heart . . .

(*Unnoticed*, GEORGIE *and* GOLDTOOTH *run noiselessly in from the right. They throw themselves upon* GAI, *who is asleep, throttling him and beating him.* KHOMICH *is the first to spot them. He rushes out left, stopping on the way only to look over his shoulder.* GRANYA *utters a short cry.* SHUROCHKA *screams, waking everybody up. The "drudge" prisoners get up, but no one dares come near enough to fight. Some of them pretend to fall asleep again*)

GRANYA: Don't just stand there! Save him! Save your gang leader! Lousy politicals, get up!

(GRANYA *grabs one of the professional crooks. Wheezing, groaning and incoherent shouts as they fight. Slowly and with a painful effort* GAI *struggles up, whereupon all four of them fall in a disorderly heap*

*towards the right, disappearing off stage. The rest just stay there,
watching.* SCHUROCHKA *screams again and again.*

A powerful blow sends GEORGIE *flying back on stage and
sprawling on to the floor.* GOLDTOOTH *retreats, pursued by* GAI,
*who keeps hitting him with a short thick wooden plank, until he falls
down on the slag between the beams, trying unsuccessfully to rise.*
GRANYA *follows* GAI *on to the stage, reeling as she walks.* GAI
*stands between the two men, who are now lying on the ground.
Exhausted and out of breath, he strikes first one and then the other
lazily about the head. The board breaks and* GAI *tries to find another,
but at that moment* LENNIE *rushes on stage from the left. He runs
like a ballet dancer, jumps easily over a sitting "drudge" prisoner,
turning the peak of his cap to the back as he flies through the air.*
GRANYA *just has time to shout* "Behind you!" *And* GAI *just has
time to turn as* LENNIE *runs into him. They both roll on the ground.
They jump up when they are almost by the parapet on the back wall
and each tries to push the other off the roof. Stunned and covered
with blood,* GOLDTOOTH *sits on the ground.* GEORGIE *gets up
with a knife in his hand and takes aim to throw it at* GAI'S *back.*
GRANYA *strikes him on the head with a board. She picks up
the knife which he has dropped, and runs up the ramp to the left-hand
pillar.* GEORGIE *pushes her in the back with a long board from
below.* GRANYA *almost falls down but then grabs the board and
they fight over it)*

LENNIE: Fascist bastard!

GAI: Who's a fascist? Who's a bastard?

*(They fall to the ground and struggle by the parapet on the wall.
The cradle of the hoist-crane is hanging beside the wall, indicating
its edge.* GOLDTOOTH *gets up, picks up a crowbar and walks
towards them, but at that moment* CHEGENYOV, *wearing torn
overalls and cocked cap, rushes on stage from the right. He sums up
the situation at a glance, overtakes* GOLDTOOTH *and grabs the*

crowbar out of his hands as he swings to strike GAI. *He hits* GOLDTOOTH *with the crowbar, who shrieks and falls to the ground.* GEORGIE *turns round, leaves* GRANYA *and throws himself at* CHEGENYOV, *who swings the crowbar violently at him.* GEORGIE *dodges the blow, they collide and roll on the floor.* GAI *grabs* LENNIE *by the throat with both hands, pushes him over the wall and holds him there in mid-air.*)

GAI: Shall I drop you? How about that, bastard? Three floors down, how about that? Who's a fascist? Come on, who's a fascist? (*He pulls* LENNIE *by the throat up on to the wall and leaves him on the parapet. Meanwhile* GRANYA *has got down from the pillar and run along the wall, which is in the process of being demolished. She throws* GAI *the knife*)

GRANYA: Pavel! Catch!

GAI: (*Catches the knife*) How about that for a toothpick?

(GOLDTOOTH *gets up.* GRANYA *jumps down on him from the wall and knocks him off his feet. Meanwhile,* GEORGIE *has overpowered* CHEGENYOV *and is throttling him.* GAI *runs up to them, pushes* GEORGIE *down, stands over him and brandishes the knife over him*) All right, start praying to your god, Mister "pro".

GEORGIE: (*In a nasty voice*) Forgive me! Forgive me!

LENNIE: (*Sits down*) All right, Pavel, we'll be friends. We'll make peace. Thieves' honour! Cross my heart and hope to rot in jail.

GAI: (*Looks triumphantly down at the three of them*) I see ... social allies, is that right? Your noble work of honour? (*To* GEORGIE *and* GOLDTOOTH. *Pointing to the right*) Over there we have four hundred bricks. By the end of dinner break they'll be on the site and ready for laying. (*Points off stage to the left*) Forward march!

(GOLDTOOTH *and* GEORGIE *take their barrow and leave the stage to the right.* CHEGENYOV *sits there trying to get his breath back*)

GAI: (*To* CHEGENYOV) Thanks, Cossack.

LENNIE: (*Feeling his neck*) You've got hands like pincers.

GAI: Attacking a man when he's asleep—how's that for your code, your thieves' honour?

LENNIE: I wasn't here when they attacked you.

GAI: Lucky for you. Otherwise I would have dropped you over the wall. You're their number one man, you'd better give them a political lecture.

LENNIE: It's all over. We're friends, didn't you hear? (*To the bricklayers, shaking his fist*) All right, you peasants, keep your mouths shut. Don't tell anyone what happened! (*Exit right*)

SHUROCHKA: (*To* GAI, *reverently, as if praying*) You're a hero, Mr Gai. A classical hero!

GAI: Bastards! If I hadn't been asleep I'd have beaten them to pulp.

(*He is still out of breath, one hand drooping at his side, holding the knife.* GRANYA *comes up to him from behind, puts her arms around him and her head on his shoulder.* GEORGIE *and* GOLDTOOTH *emerge from the right pushing a barrow with about fifty bricks in it. As they cross the stage the painted curtain falls*)

Act III, Scene 3

The Concert

(*A large spacious room with a temporary floor and walls which have been made good but not yet plastered. In the back wall there are two tall windows; outside the night is very dark. The room is brightly lit. A few small steps by the left wall lead up to the door, which leads on to the 'stage'. A small screen, part of the set for a play, stands closer to the audience, screening off the place where women change. Next to the screen, almost by the proscenium, is a bench set against the wall. On the bench sit* NEMOV, *in his black camp uniform, and* LYUBA, *dressed up to take part in the performance. It is a busy room, full of bustle and coming and going. People are changing clothes and rehearsing and looking for things they need for the play. They keep rushing out on to the 'stage' and returning. Occasionally the 'stage' door is left open. When this happens one can hear snatches of a farcical sketch. The characters are: a stupid German officer, played by* KOSTYA *the work allocator; his idiot of a batman; an old woman wearing a kerchief; her daughter, a member of the underground, played by* SHUROCHKA; *her grandson, a young pioneer, played by* DIMKA; *a frightening-looking guerrilla figure in a black beard, who comes on to the 'stage' only towards the end of the play.*

*There is a small light-music band (*ZHENKA *among them) huddled together on the right at the back of the stage. They are trying to rehearse quietly, but the result is rather loud.* VITKA, *the quick-moving, red-haired compère of the show, is rushing about more than anybody else*)

COMPERE: (*To the group*) All right, boys, that's enough.

SOMEONE: What about supper, Vitka? Do the actors get supper?
COMPERE: I hear the cook's in the accounts department. (*He runs off. Enter* GONTOIR)
GONTOIR: (*In a tired voice*) Young man, take this gun.
(DIMKA *walks off carrying the dummy gun*)
ZHENKA: (*Clears his throat and starts to sing*)
Coming home on a prayer and a wing . . .
KOSTYA: (*His voice audible from the 'stage'*) Ich vill shoot you all, russische Schweine.
COMPERE: (*Rushing in*) Where's the bucket? Come on, we must have the bucket. (*A 'prop' bucket is produced*)
SOMEONE: Let's hear it again, Vitka. Who comes after who?
COMPERE: Zhenka, I've had a note from the lieutenant. The song of the American bomber pilot has to be cut.
ZHENKA: Why? They're our allies, aren't they?
COMPERE: Don't ask me. They *were* our allies, but don't ask questions. Just give them "The Blue Scarf"—loud as you can. (*Shouts*) Can I have your attention! The "Stupid German" sketch is about to finish. The band will now play "Song of the Motherland". Then Lyuba, then Zhenka with his "Blue Scarf", then Dimka's Cossack dancing, then Lyuba again. Then the band plays the march and falls out. After that the play *Sheep and Wolves*.
(*Buzz of voices from the actors*)
SHUROCHKA: (*To* GONTOIR) Well, how is it going? (*Loud applause from the audience*)
GONTOIR: You can hear for yourself . . . "Licensed for performance in corrective labour camps"—that's the sort of play it is.
COMPERE: I know nothing about it, nothing at all! (*Rushes out*)
VOICE FROM THE STAGE: You think because I am an old woman that I am afraid of your tanks? Grandson, translate into German for him—long live the collective farms! (*Applause*)

GONTOIR: (*He speaks without the slightest foreign accent*) Is this the kind of art we used to dream about? We were so enthusiastic back in 1919. We came to young Russia to create the neo-theatre, the first in the history of mankind.

> Turn their rainbow to a yoke,
> Make harness of the Milky Way,
> Renew for us our earthly sphere
> So it may see a brighter day . . . .

(*He sits down and starts putting on his make-up to play a part in* Sheep and Wolves. SHUROCHKA *walks out on to the stage*)

ZHENKA: (*Sings sadly*) Coming home on a prayer and a wing . . .

LYUBA: I was six. I remember a huge barge full of dispossessed *kulak* farmers. There were no partitions in the hold, no tiered bunks. People just lay on top of other people. Maybe it was because I was small, but the walls of the barge seemed to tower over me like cliffs. Guards with guns walked round the top edge. Our whole family was exiled, but our two elder brothers weren't living with us, so they weren't touched. They came to the transit camp. The boat had just left and they tried to catch up with us. All the time they were on the look-out for a chance to get their family out of trouble. They didn't succeed. But they managed to buy me from the escort commander. They gave him a shirt with a zip—they were just coming into fashion. I don't remember how they got me off the barge, but I remember we were in a little boat, and the water shone brightly in the sun.

NEMOV: What about your parents?

LYUBA: They died up beyond the Arctic Circle. They starved to death. They were dumped in the naked tundra. How could they survive?

COMPERE: Pay attention, everyone! Official communiqué—our supper has been approved. Contents will be clarified later.

(*The band plays a muted flourish*)

LYUBA: You can't imagine how we lived after that. I had no room, so I lived five years in a bit of dark corridor. There was no window and I couldn't do my homework after school. I went to school every day hungry and dressed like a beggar. I couldn't complain or ask for help in case people found out we were *kulaks*. But I wanted pretty dresses. I wanted to go to the cinema . . . My brother married. He has his own children . . . They married me off when I was fourteen . . .

NEMOV: Fourteen?

(*The sketch has finished. Noise and movement.* SHUROCHKA *rushes behind the screen to change*)

COMPERE: Musicians, on stage! Come on, Lyuba, get ready.

VOICES: You missed out a whole passage.

I come back to it later.

Where's the vaseline?

Who's the pig who's been sitting on my dress?

Oh, it's so hot!

(*The "old woman" from the sketch, her kerchief slipped to one side, jumps on to the table, sits down on it and cheekily lights up a cigarette. She says to the musicians* "Hi, hooligans!")

DIMKA: (*To* GONTOIR) Didn't I learn my part well, sir?

SOMEONE: Hey, what are you doing in the camps? You're too young!

DIMKA: I escaped from trade school. They wouldn't give us anything to eat.

SOMEONE: You're worse off here than you were there.

DIMKA: No! I get good rations now. I've learnt about life.

GONTOIR: (*Putting on his make-up*) What do you mean—life?

DIMKA: Life's when you don't have to sweat your guts out. Let the others sweat their guts out. (*He is changing into Cossack boy's dress for his dance.* SHUROCHKA *comes out from behind the screen dressed as a nineteenth-century middle-class young lady. She is to play* GLAFIRA *in* Sheep and Wolves)

SHUROCHKA: (*Quoting from her part*) "What have you done with me? I'm so nervous, I'm so nervous!"

NEMOV: (*Holding* LYUBA *back*) Wait another minute.

LYUBA: (*Indicating her dress*) Does it suit me?

NEMOV: Everything suits you.

LYUBA: I love acting and dressing up. It's wonderful wearing a new outfit for every turn.

COMPERE: Lyuba, come on! How many more times?

(LYUBA *runs off.* NEMOV *watches her go*)

SHUROCHKA: (*Putting on her make-up, to* NEMOV) Did you hear the way Gontoir read Tolstoy?

NEMOV: What did you say?

SHUROCHKA: What are you smiling at?

NEMOV: Smiling?

SHUROCHKA: It made me sad. They chattered all the way through, no one paid attention. There were only one or two in the whole audience who appreciated how well he did it. You didn't hear it either. It was from *War and Peace*, the bit about the oak-tree.

NEMOV: (*Warming to the idea*) The bit about the black oak-tree which turned green?

GONTOIR: (*Coming up to them*) You see, I'm incorrigible. I insist on believing that beauty elevates human beings. I keep wanting to cheer them up, to tell them there is more to life than work parades, searches and prison soup.

COMPERE: All right, "Blue Scarf"! Get ready! Everyone pay attention! The extra supper has been positively confirmed—one jam-roll, two spoonfuls of boiled rice for each person!

SHUROCHKA: Rice? You must be mad! Rice doesn't exist!

SOMEONE: What the hell's rice?

(COMPERE *walks quickly off stage, leaving the door open. We can hear* LYUBA *finishing her song.*

LYUBA: "For you I have but one request:
     Do not put me to the test.
     You may dance at my wedding, for sure,
     But do not expect anything more."

(*Loud and prolonged applause, shouts of* "Encore". LYUBA *appears in the doorway, but then goes back on to the* "*stage*")

SHUROCHKA: Monsieur Gontoir, have you heard the rumour? They say in a few days there's going to be a big transport, for the fifty-eighters.

GONTOIR: It's quite possible. They often do it before Revolution Day. But these rumours don't mean much. There're always rumours.

SHUROCHKA: I just don't have the strength. I couldn't stand a winter in a new place. Why do they torment us like this, moving us on all the time?

(LYUBA *rushes in. She reaches the spot where* NEMOV *is sitting, then runs away again. Applause*)

GONTOIR: I heard something different. I heard that just before we arrived they arrested a young poet—I mean, they threw him in the cooler. One of the assistant doctors found some verses under his pillow. He's under investigation. They say he's dying. Have you heard anything about it?

(*Applause.* LYUBA *comes back, her face shining, her movements quick and impetuous*)

SHUROCHKA: Congratulations, Lyuba. You sounded just like Shulzhenko.

LYUBA: Did I? You noticed, did you? Everyone says I'm like her. I was in key, wasn't I? I was frightened I wouldn't get it right. I have to change now. (*To* NEMOV) Come on, you can help me. Quick! (*She runs behind the screen. Her naked arm appears from time to time from behind the screen to hand* NEMOV *a piece of clothing or to take one which* NEMOV *has selected from the pile of clothes on the bench)*

LYUBA: (*From behind the screen*) Here, take this . . . put that down . . . I want the one under the blue thing . . . Be careful with it, remember none of it's mine. I borrowed it from those women outside camp. Come on, you can button me up. Come here. (NEMOV *goes around to the other side of the screen, so that the audience cannot see him. The screen is then turned so that* LYUBA *and* NEMOV *can be seen by the audience although not by the other characters on stage.* LYUBA *is looking at herself in a little mirror.* NEMOV *buttons up her dress from behind, kisses her neck, embraces her and turns her round to face him. A long kiss)*

NEMOV: Lyubonka, what's happening to me?

LYUBA: What indeed? (*They kiss*)

NEMOV: Who taught you to kiss like that?

LYUBA: I learnt . . . (*They kiss*)

NEMOV: Lyuba, you're . . . you're a desperate woman. You seem to drink me in, swallow me. I won't be without you now, do you hear me? I can't be without you . . .

LYUBA: We only got to know each other today, and you say you can't live without me?

NEMOV: Ever since I was arrested I've felt as if I was living in a cloud of black smoke. I haven't been able to smile. But it's so wonderful now, now I'm with you. It's as if you've released me, let me out into freedom.

LYUBA: Go on talking.

NEMOV: You told me about that barge and that dark corridor where you lived. It made me feel you were my little sister, and you'd been hurt. And now suddenly those unbelievable kisses, and the way you tremble in my arms. I've . . . I've fallen in love with you, Lyubonka.

LYUBA: How can you? You're married.

NEMOV: My wife's ten years **away,** a hundred fences of barbed wire away. I can hardly imagine she exists.

LYUBA: You don't know much about me. My first husband used to beat me and I left him. My second husband was a complete waster. When I was arrested he renounced me. Ever since then . . .

NEMOV: You poor girl . . .

LYUBA: I am not a poor girl at all. You see, I've had lovers . . . More than one.

NEMOV: (*Starts*) How many?

LYUBA: More than one. You can't possibly love me.

NEMOV: But Lyuba, you had to do it, isn't that right? It wasn't because you wanted it was it?

LYUBA: But what if I did want it? You think it has no effect on a girl, getting married when she's fourteen?

NEMOV: Lyuba, it couldn't have been for that they saved you from that prison barge?

LYUBA: (*Putting her arms around his neck*) You're so kind to me. Why didn't I meet you earlier?

COMPERE: Lyuba, where are you? Get on stage!

LYUBA: (*Kisses* NEMOV *once more*) I'm coming!

(*Slowly and unwillingly she walks away.* NEMOV *sits down on the bench and runs his fingers through the dress* LYUBA *has just taken off. In a far corner someone is quietly playing the guitar*)

SHUROCHKA: (*Aiming her words at* NEMOV, *very distinctly*) "I have told you that love will bring you nothing but suffering". (NEMOV *turns round and looks at her*) I am rehearsing my part, it's my part. Ostrovsky wrote it. You look radiant, as if you'd been given the key to heaven. I envy you, I do really.

NEMOV: I envy myself.

SHUROCHKA: (*Leaning towards him*) Do you know everything about Lyuba?

NEMOV: (*Pronouncing every syllable separately*) I don't want to know anything.

(SCHUROCHKA *moves away. We can hear* LYUBA *singing.* KOSTYA *comes up to* NEMOV, *his make-up almost completely removed. He is wearing his usual military uniform*)

KOSTYA: (*To* NEMOV) Well, how's life? I see you're not missing any chances?

NEMOV: How's *your* life?

KOSTYA: Same as ever. A bit screwed up, though. I've had a row with the skivers. That bastard Rubyan keeps laying traps for me. Khomich is playing the great man. I got into a bit of a mess over you as well. I didn't think you'd get the push as soon as that. In fact, I reckon I've burnt my fingers. (*He moves away. Loud, stormy applause.* LYUBA *returns, but not immediately, only when the band starts playing a march. She sits down silently next to* NEMOV. *He takes her by the hand*)

COMPERE: All right, Gontoir, *Sheep and Wolves*. Ready for the kick-off! Well done, Lyuba, superb! Even the commandant applauded! (*Runs off*)

LYUBA: Why didn't you come out and hear me sing!

NEMOV: Where can we meet? I mean, on our own?

LYUBA: No, perhaps we'd better not.

NEMOV: We must, we must. I can't tear myself away from you now.

LYUBA: (*Sighs*) Look, wouldn't it be better if I stayed your sister? I'll be a good sister, you'll see.

NEMOV: No. (*He looks around, pulls* LYUBA *behind the screen and they kiss*) When I kiss you I feel I want to die. Where did you learn to kiss like that?

LYUBA: (*Caressing him*) If only I could change back again, just
for you. Become clean and pure.

NEMOV: Where can we meet? Where?

LYUBA: All right, I'll come to the foundry. To the attic where
they store the coke. (*Pause*) Do we really have to? Do we? (*They
come and sit down on the bench*) What do you think will happen?
Have you thought about that? (*With sudden fervour*)Darling, tell
me one thing. Are you hungry? I mean now? Because I am. All my
life I've been hungry. How will we be able to survive this camp?
You'll never be able to fix things up for yourself, you haven't got
a trade. By yourself you might be able to keep afloat, but with me
round your neck you'll sink. In a little while you'll want to get
rid of me.

NEMOV: No! Never!

LYUBA: The foreman will kick me out. I'll be on general
duties . . .

NEMOV: (*In alarm*) Why did the foreman take you as a runner?

LYUBA: It's what happens in the camps. Everyone does it.

NEMOV: So you and he have . . .

LYUBA: No, not yet. He doesn't have time. The telephone keeps
ringing.

NEMOV: But what if he finds time? Tomorrow, say?

LYUBA: Will you be able to find me another job, one as good as
that?

NEMOV: Lyuba, as from today . . .

LYUBA: What do you want of me? Don't you understand?
I'm what prisoners call a "love-girl". Do you know what that
means? I'm a "love-girl".

(*The members of the band burst into the room. A din of voices. They
put down their instruments.* GONTOIR *and* SHUROCHKA *walk on
to the stage.* KOLODEY, KHOMICH *and* MERESHCHUN *walk
in from the opposite direction*)

KOLODEY: (*To* GONTOIR) What a sight! You look like a circus clown. Is it a funny play?

GONTOIR: Very funny.

KOLODEY: O.K., we'll laugh. Why shouldn't we laugh, we're off duty? That stuff you did earlier all about the oak-trees and the fir-trees, it went on and on. Everyone's sick of timber-felling anyway. (GONTOIR *walks away.* MERESHCHUN *laughs loudly*) I mean it. What's in an oak-tree? Four cubic metres. that's all. But he went on and on . . .

KHOMICH: Where is she? Where is the seductress? Lyuba, you sang brilliantly. You look like you're on your way to a state banquet. You heard how they clapped, you might have been a Hollywood star. Even the commandant had to applaud. Congratulations (*He shakes her hand*)

KOLODEY: (*Walking round the room*) Well, how are you all doing? Breaking any rules?

MERESHCHUN: Lyuba, you sang with such fire, such expression! (*He shakes her hand and sits down on the bench next to her, on the other side from* NEMOV) I once heard Shulzhenko sing. You're just as good as she is. I'd like to send a telegram to Sochi and order a bouquet of flowers for you—by special plane.

LYUBA: (*Flattered*) Thank you, thank you.

MERESHCHUN: (*Takes her by the elbow*) Why don't you ever come to the hospital? I could give you a couple of days sick leave before Revolution Day. Would you like that?

LYUBA: What for? I'm not ill.

MERESHCHUN: What do you mean, what for? Women always have things to do—washing their hair or their clothes. You come to the hospital tomorrow, I'll see you're let off work. Will you?

KHOMICH: Well, Nemov, how do you find work in the foundry? Not so good? You know, I spent days trying to think of some job we could give you. I couldn't think of anything.

NEMOV: Thank you, but I asked for nothing better.

KHOMICH: Maybe so, but educated men should behave like gentlemen. We should help each other out in time of trouble . . . (*He spots* ZHENKA) Hey, mister, you sing like an angel. Why don't you ever sing classical music?

ZHENKA: I wrote a letter home. I asked them to send me Tchaikovsky . . .

KHOMICH: Why Tchaikovsky? Why not "The Gypsy Baron" or "The Blue Mazurka"?

COMPERE: All those who want to hear the play—it's time to join the audience. We're starting now.

(KHOMICH *and most of the actors leave*)

KOLODEY: Don't start yet. Wait for me. (*To* NEMOV) What are you doing here? Stand up when you're spoken to. (NEMOV *stands up*) What are you on?

NEMOV: Nothing, citizen commander. I simply happen to be here.

KOLODEY: Nothing's ever simple with you prisoners. You've always got ideas in the back of your heads. Get out into the audience, you're not an actor.

NEMOV: What does it matter, sir? Can't I watch the play from here?

KOLODEY: You're not allowed to watch from here. When you're production chief, all right, fine, watch from wherever you like. Only you're not production chief now, you're a "drudge" prisoner, isn't that right? You've had your sugar. Go on, get out there.

NEMOV: Please, sir, let me stay here.

KOLODEY: (*Becoming angry*) I said it's not allowed. We're on the edge of the camp zone. How do I know you're not planning to go over the fence? Go on, or I'll have you in the cooler. (NEMOV *walks off, turning back to look at* LYUBA) Doctor!

MERESHCHUN: (*Without getting up*) What is it, boss?

KOLODEY: (*Quietly*) Do you have any alcohol in your hospital?

MERESHCHUN: No, I don't. But for you—maybe! I'll see what I can do.

KOLODEY: I just want a bit for myself. A hundred grammes or so. I'll call in after the concert.

MERESHCHUN: Fine.

KOLODEY: All right, time to start, is it? Let's go in and have a laugh. (*He leaves. The words of the play can only faintly be heard. There are very few people left in the room*)

MERESHCHUN: Lyuba, I was a colonel in the army, I was divisional medical officer. Life inside was harder for me to get used to than for the others. I had a taste of general duties— thirty days. My feet swelled up so much I couldn't take my boots off. So I gave in. Now you wouldn't get me out of my hospital for all the gold in Christendom. You see, Lyuba, in these camps hospital is the key—the key to everything! I can fix you up in my hospital as a food orderly.

LYUBA: I'm fixed up already.

MERESHCHUN: You're a runner, aren't you? Big deal! I could fix you up so that you wouldn't need to leave camp until the end of your term. I'm not much of a talker, but I've really put down roots in this place. They're more likely to post the commandant than they are to post me. You think I want you just for one night? No, Lyuba, I don't. We'll live together properly—man and wife. (LYUBA *says nothing*) I've just received a food parcel. (*He takes her hands in his*) How many years has it been since you ate a cake, a real cake with chocolate icing? And real sausage! And American corned beef! It's like a dream, isn't it?

LYUBA: (*Taking her hands away from his*) I'm very happy for you, doctor. But eat it with someone else, not with me.

MERESHCHUN: Lyuba, I'd rather eat it with you. (*He embraces her*)

LYUBA: (*In a faint voice*) You see, doctor, you're irresistible. You can have any woman in the camp. I'm not the only woman in the world. It's so hard for me, listening to what you say . . . (*She extricates herself from his arms and sits there gloomily. A single musician is producing sad sounds on a wind instrument. The painted curtain falls*)

(*During the interval sentries are changed on the towers as before. The guards to be mounted march across the front of the stalls, moving on any members of the audience who happen to be there*)

Act IV, Scene 1

The Bronze is Flowing

(*The foundry. The bronze furnace has been rebuilt. Occasionally a small flame can be seen in it through a chink.* MUNITSA *and* YAKHIMCHUK *are standing next to the furnace.* MUNITSA *is fussing around. He keeps peering inside the furnace through the window.* YAKHIMCHUK *is reserved. There are a few prepared moulds standing next to the furnace.* NEMOV *is mixing the moulding earth with a spade. The door of the dryer is wide open.* CHEGENYOV *is sorting out some rubbish on the roof of the dryer*)

MUNITSA: She melt! The bastard, she melt! (*He dances up and down*) Fifteen minutes more and bronze come, first-class bronze!
CHEGENYOV: Bronze'll come all right, now grandad's shown you how to do it.
MUNITSA: He don't know so much. (*Indicating* YAKHIMCHUK) I build better than what he build. I know burner gotta be small.
YAKHIMCHUK: Then why are you such a fool, why couldn't you work it out for yourself? Why did your bronze burn away till nothing was left?
CHEGENYOV: (*Sorting out the rubbish*) Fittings, tubings, mouldings—look at it! God knows what we'd do if we didn't have holidays to sort it out. Well, I've had enough, I don't care if we need it or not, it's all going into the furnace. Then we'll have a bit of order.
(*Enter* LYUBA *from the left wearing a buttoned-up quilt jacket. The door behind her slams noisily*)

LYUBA: Is Kuznetsov here? (*The foundry workers are busy and do not answer.* LYUBA *makes a sign to* NEMOV *and walks slowly towards the dryer.* NEMOV *follows her. They stand in the doorway of the dryer, which gapes darkly, as wide as a cave. They talk quietly*)

NEMOV: What is it?

LYUBA: (*very upset*) Darling! (*She embraces him*) I came just in case to say . . . to say goodbye!

NEMOV: A transport? Is that it?

LYUBA: Yes.

NEMOV: Wait a minute, maybe we can . . . Maybe they won't . . .

LYUBA: You think that doctor will put up with things the way they are? It had to be one of us—either you or me. (*Pause*) Have you been happy this week . . . our week together?

NEMOV: (*Stroking her face*) It was so good . . . I was so happy . . .

LYUBA: I'm so grateful to you too. I'll keep this last week as long as I live, hidden deep inside me.

NEMOV: Is there nothing we can do?

LYUBA: (*Excitedly*) There is something! We can stay! We can even love one another—secretly, very secretly. Only you must promise . . . you must agree . . . to share me. You must share me with the doctor. I'll bring you things to eat.

NEMOV: Could you do that?

LYUBA: Yes, I could! Couldn't you? My dear little brother, couldn't you accept it? Why should you have to leave? At least I'd be able to see you from a distance maybe, but . . .

NEMOV: (*Hugging her*) Lyuba, I could never share you, not the smallest piece of you, with anyone.

LYUBA: (*She frees herself from him and speaks very sadly*) Well, you must give me up, then. You'll lose all of me, all of me. (*She walks slowly back towards the main exit. The door slams and in runs* DIMKA, *in a happy mood*)

DIMKA: Hurray! It's up in the main building. They've turned the star on! Hurray! (*He runs round in a full circle, almost knocking* LYUBA *off her feet and then runs out. The door slams.* NEMOV *does not move.* LYUBA *opens the door and walks out. The door slams*)

CHEGENYOV: (*Squatting on top of the dryer, he looks out through the top window in the direction indicated by* DIMKA. *From the top of the dryer he addresses the company in the manner of a public speaker*) Comrades, your attention! Today's anniversary will be celebrated in our camp with particular solemnity. Items on the agenda. Number one—the superb work and valiant exploits of Munitsa. Number two—the despatch of forty or fifty trouble-makers to the forests to chop down trees.

YAKHIMCHUK: You watch it with your forecasts. They'll come true.

CHEGENYOV: Number three—Old Igor has been transferred to the morgue after being stuck with a bayonet to make sure he was dead. Number four—there will be a general search in all barrack-rooms, mattresses turned over and floors taken up. Number five—there will be a personal search at the check-point. Under-pants will be removed. Number six—there will be a Stakhanovite rally of the best "drudge" prisoners. Each Stakhanovite will be issued with one millet pasty, which means the rest of the camp have to take a cut in flour and millet next week. Number seven— there will be a free film-show, *Stalin in 1905.* Everyone will fight to get in and will end up sitting on everyone else, to make sure we don't feel we're at home. (*He jumps astride some suitable object*) Mount your horses! Sabres at the ready! Charge! (*He makes a mock cavalry charge, waving an imaginary sabre. His elbows are sticking out of the holes in his sleeves*)

YAKHIMCHUK: You bum, you'll get yourself into the glass-house.

CHEGENYOV: Stuff that, grandpa. Do you think I care about the damn foundry? If they'd given me *five* years, all right, I wouldn't have minded slaving a bit. But fifteen! Can you imagine—fifteen! I'll take the rest of my term in travel rations from the Big Boss himself.

MUNITSA: What do you mean, travel rations?

CHEGENYOV: (*Indicating the end of his finger*) Nine grammes. (*Pause*) Lead injection. (*He points the finger at his head, then lets his head droop as if he was dead.*

(*Enter* KAPLYUZHNIKOV, *a neatly dressed, portly fellow wearing a fine fur coat, together with* GURVICH *and* BRYLOV. *The wind, noisier than before, slams the door behind them, They do not notice* CHEGENYOV, *who quietly takes up a position as if he was working. He does some more tidying up on the dryer and then jumps down.*

NEMOV *carries on with his spade, shovelling the moulding earth*)

BRYLOV: You see, comrade chief engineer, Brylov always keeps his word. I said you'd have bronze, and you have bronze. I understand the situation. Your excavators are at a standstill. So I have used my initiative.

GURVICH: Who's used his initiative? We'll soon see about that. You've put so many spanners in my works ...

BRYLOV: Comrade Gurvich, how could you say such a thing? Strike a good horse with one hand, yes, but you should wipe away its tears with the other. All you do is hand orders while I rack my brains over your furnace. Ask the boys, if you don't believe me.

MUNITSA: (*Roars with laughter and slaps his thigh*) Five minutes more, then bronze come. I know about working in foundry.

YAKHIMCHUK: (*Leaning against his slag-scrubber as if it was a long sword*) Much better show the boss your trousers, Munitsa.

(MUNITSA *shows* GURVICH *his trousers. They are in tatters.*)

KAPLYUZHNIKOV: (*To* GURVICH) Why don't you issue them with overalls? Seriously

GURVICH: You must know why, comrade. Head Office don't have funds.

KAPLYUZHNIKOV: No funds? Write to camp centre, then. Maybe they'll find something.

YAKHIMCHUK: Why should they? And there's another thing— ours is a high-temperature workshop. We're workers like anyone else. Why don't they give us a milk ration? Workers outside get it.

KAPLYUZHNIKOV: (*Quite astounded*) Milk? You want milk? Whatever next? Tea and biscuits in bed, I suppose! (*Reaction*) You see, comrades—I mean citizens, not comrades—you see, citizens, if we did that where would it stop? I don't know . . . the milk situation's a bit difficult at the moment. Do you see?

YAKHIMCHUK: Of course, citizen commander, we see. One step to the right or left and the escort guard will open fire.

KAPLYUZHNIKOV: (*Pretending he hasn't quite heard*) Gurvich, when will the beams be ready? And the plates?

GURVICH: (*To* BRYLOV) What's happened to the cast-iron? Why hasn't any been moulded?

BRYLOV: Yakhimchuk, what about this cast-iron? Has it been hoisted?

YAKHIMCHUK: It's no problem hoisting it. That's just two day's work. But who's going to mould it?

BRYLOV: (*To* GURVICH) Chegenyov has been moulding the simpler stuff. Munitsa's been busy with the bronze. He hasn't got two pairs of hands.

GURVICH: (*To* KAPLYUZHNIKOV) The iron's been held up by the bronze.

KAPLYUZHNIKOV: Come, comrades, this won't do at all. Our production line must deliver *all* the goods, the bronze *and* the iron. If you succeed with the bronze, we give you a pat on the back. But if you fail with the iron, we put you on a charge. Any complaints?

GURVICH: (*To* BRYLOV) We must have the iron in three days, and that's that. What's the bronze got to do with it? If Munitsa doesn't have enough time, all right, he can do his mouldings in the evenings or on holidays. I'll see he gets a special escort guard.

BRYLOV: Well, Munitsa, that's the score. You've got two days. You'll spend your holiday here and do the moulding. (*To* YAKHIMCHUK) As for you, why aren't you hoisting the iron? You're spoilt, that's what's wrong.

YAKHIMCHUK: Dimka! . . . Where is that devil of a boy? (DIMKA *appears*) You and Nemov go and deal with the iron. Pull it up in the bucket. I'll do the bronze and join you later. (*To* GURVICH) You ought to have a protective fence put there. (NEMOV *and* DIMKA *go out of the back door*)

GURVICH: (*To* BRYLOV) Your foundrymen are a bit work-shy these days. What's wrong? Rates too high? We can easily lower them.

BRYLOV: Don't you touch the rates.

GURVICH: Why not? Because you live off them too, is that it?

KAPLYUZHNIKOV: Of course we'll revise the rates. Making bronze—that's a wounderful Revolution Day present. I'll send a telegram to headquarters. (*Takes* GURVICH *to the front of the stage.* BRYLOV *creeps up beside them, trying to overhear what they are saying and to interrupt. From time to time one can hear, from the room above, the sound of pieces of iron being thrown on the sheet-iron ceiling of the workshop*) We must get the furnace documented, apply for a patent. It's an invention! Yours and mine! (GURVICH *tries to draw* KAPLYUZHNIKOV *away from* BRYLOV, *but* BRYLOV *keeps following them*) We'll have to accept Brylov as co-owner.

GURVICH: But he didn't do a thing. He just got in the way.

KAPLYUZHNIKOV: You don't understand, he's got connections in personnel. He'll denounce us all, he'll make a real nuisance of himself. There's good money here. I've had a word with the trade-union committee. We'll arrange a bonus system—a few thousand roubles each. Free holidays as well maybe. (*He nods to* BRYLOV *to join them. The three heads are put together in a whispering huddle. Meanwhile* YAKHIMCHUK *and* CHEGENYOV *carry a bucket over to the furnace and fix it on a two-pronged support.* MUNITSA *is fussing around the furnace, peering in its window*)

MUNITSA: Yes! One second! One second and she come!

(BRYLOV *walks away from the two engineers and towards the furnace*)

GURVICH: Yes, sir, I know it's against safety rules, I've got common sense the same as the next man. But how can we build a fence if the office won't let us have any planks? They've already used more construction materials than they're allowed.

KAPLYUZHNIKOV: You must find some, then. You must find some.

GURVICH: You know the way I work: a hundred telephone calls a day, instructors and inspectors calling on me three times a week, every other day committee meetings at Head Office. I'm supposed to prepare documents and reports for them, and at the same time someone has to take care of our production. The foremen are all drunk, the rate-fixing office is full of prisoners I can't trust, I have to check all the rates. The volume of work's always being increased, and every minute I hear some job's been bungled somewhere, or pipes laid in the wrong place, which means that ditches have to be dug open. I'm worse off than a prisoner. I come home in the evening, I don't even want to look at my wife . . .

KAPLYUZHNIKOV: What can we do? I have five hundred documents a week I'm supposed to sign. It's not easy for me either. (*He leaves towards the right. Through the left-hand door walks* KOSTYA *the work allocator, carrying a list in his hand. He is followed by a group of prisoners already dressed in winter clothes— quilted jackets and ear-flap hats. The wind slams the door repeatedly, making banging sounds like shots. There is anxious murmuring among those who have just come in*)

VOICE: Who's going? Who else has been posted?

VOICE: Kostya, where are they taking us?

KOSTYA: The Crimean riviera, of course!

VOICE: Am I in it or aren't I?

KOSTYA: Stop yelling, or someone will get it in the neck. Haven't any of you been on a transport before? There's a hell of a gale outside, I couldn't hold my list properly. (*To* CHEGENYOV, *who has just approached him*) Where's Nemov?

CHEGENYOV: Is he posted?

KOSTYA: He was on the list, but the hospital crossed him out. Just a minute ago. (*He leaves, followed by a crowd of prisoners*)

VOICE: If it's red wagons, they cut off all our buttons.

VOICE: If its old goods wagons, they'll smash our suitcases.

VOICE: I hear they're taking us to Vorkuta.

VOICE: It's a lousy life, being a prisoner.

(*More threatening pistol-shots sound as the door slams.* GURVICH *and* KAPLYUZHNIKOV *return from the right*)

BRYLOV: (*By the furnace*) All right, Munitsa, it's ready! Let it out!

MUNITSA: Right now! (*He strikes a hole. A stream of bronze pours down the shute into the bucket*)

YAKHIMCHUK *and* BRYLOV: (*Together*) That's enough! Stop! Watch the slag! That's enough!

KAPLYUZHNIKOV: No, it's not enough! We want more!

YAKHIMCHUK: (*In a commanding voice*) Close the hole! (MUNITSA *closes it*)

GURVICH: (*In a pleading voice, to* YAKHIMCHUK) Can't we get any more?

YAKHIMCHUK: No, we can't. The slag might spoil the bushes. Quality rather than quantity.

(MUNITSA *cleans the surface of the bronze.* CHEGENYOV *and* YAKHIMCHUK *carry the bucket away and pour the metal into moulds*)

BRYLOV: Excellent! Well done! We'll soon have the excavators going!

MUNITSA: (*Standing by a mould he has just filled with metal*) So what I tell you? What Munitsa tell you? We have bronze!

YAKHIMCHUK: Wait till we get it on the lathe. We'll see what sort of bronze it is.

BRYLOV: Don't spoil our holiday. It's a victory for the whole foundry.

KAPLYUZHNIKOV: Well done! Well done! I'll go and send a telegram to Head Office. (*He leaves*)

MUNITSA: (*To* BRYLOV) So, we get bonus, yes?

BRYLOV: (*Sighs*) I don't really know, Munitsa. What's the bonus for? If it was a new type of furnace, maybe we would, but we didn't invent it. It looks better than it is, but only to those who don't understand. If you weren't a prisoner, well, maybe you could put a bit of pressure on, refer it to the trade unions, to the central committee . . .

GURVICH: O.K., Munitsa, O.K., let's see the bushes. Take off the moulds.

MUNITSA: No can do. They not set yet. They have to harden. (*From the back room up above* DIMKA *is heard to utter a loud yell. For the last time we hear a lump of iron falling on the ceiling.* CHEGENYOV *rushes through the back door followed by* YAKHIMCHUK)

GURVICH: What's happened? (*He hurries after them, but bumps into* DIMKA *by the door*)

DIMKA: (*Shouts*) A lump of iron fell on his head! (*Pause while they look at him*) Nemov! Nemov's been killed! (*He rushes out, slamming the door with a noise like a pistol-shot.* CHEGENYOV *and* YAKHIMCHUK *carry* NEMOV *in, his head covered with blood. He is unconscious.* GURVICH *follows them, head bowed*)

BRYLOV: What's the matter? How did it happen?

YAKHIMCHUK: You're no foundryman, you don't know your arse from your elbow. That's what's the matter! I told you, didn't I? I said it was dangerous hoisting iron up in a bucket. (*They carry* NEMOV *out. The wind makes it difficult for them to open the door*)

MUNITSA: (*Running to catch up with* GURVICH) Sir! What about bonus? I get bonus? Yes?

GURVICH: Just look after the moulds. Take care of the iron. (*The painted curtain falls.*)

(*Before the next scene begins the lanterns on top of the barbed wire round the orchestra pit are switched on. They stay alight until the end of the performance*)

Act IV, Scene 2

The Transport

(The set as in Act I, Scene One. The wind is whining, stirring up the powdery snow. It is dusk. The inmates of the camp are crowding the work area behind the barbed wire. They stand motionless, staring towards the living area in the direction of the audience. About thirty other prisoners whose files have already been examined are sitting in the middle of the yard, right on the ground, their belongings with them, huddled together. A searchlight beam comes to rest on a newly hung placard with the slogan: "People are the most valuable capital—J. Stalin". KOLODEY is in charge of despatching the transport. He is assisted by the wardress, who has a mane of hair under her winter hat, the doctor's assistant AGA-MIRZA, KOSTYA and POSOSHKOV. The window of MERESHCHUN's cabin is lit up. He is standing at the steps, a white overcoat over his warm clothes.

The high-sided lorry, the same one as in Act I, Scene One, backs onto the stage from the right)

KOLODEY: All right, those who have been examined, single file, quick march!

(The prisoners quickly begin to climb into the back of the lorry, pushing each other aside)

ESCORT-GUARD SERGEANT: *(He is standing right in the back of the lorry behind a protective grill, armed with a sub-machine gun)* Sit down! Hurry up and sit down! On the floor, not on your bags! Don't turn round! Face the rear! No talking!

KOLODEY: *(To KOSTYA)* Who's missing?

KOSTYA: Here are the last three. Hurry up, slowcoaches!
(GONTOIR, GRANYA *and* SHUROCHKA *emerge from behind the hut on the left*)
ESCORT-GUARD SERGEANT: Gop . . . Gop. . . .
GONTOIR: Gontoir, Camille Leopoldovich, born 1890, Article 58, paragraph one A stroke nineteen. Ten years.
ESCORT-GUARD SERGEANT: Take your hat off then! (GONTOIR *bares his silvery head. The sergeant compares him with the photograph on the cover of his file*) You don't look much like your picture . . . All right, on you go. (GONTOIR *clambers into the lorry*) Soykina!
SHUROCHKA: (*Fussing over her belongings*) Soykina, Alexandra Pavlovna, Article 58, paragraph twelve. Ten years. (*She is almost crying. Her things are too heavy for her. There is no one to help her. Finally* KOSTYA *heaves her luggage into the back of the lorry*)
ESCORT-GUARD SERGEANT: Zybina!
GRANYA: (*Her voice clear and angry*) Agrafena Mikhailovna, born 1920, Article 136. Ten years.
GAI: (*Shouting from the work area*) Goodbye, Granya!
GRANYA: (*Shouts*) Goodbye, Pavel!
GAI: Write to me!
GRANYA: It's too late!
GAI: Don't give in, Granya!
GRANYA: I won't!
KOLODEY: (*Stepping in front of her*) Stop that! (*Taunting her*) Don't want to leave your lover behind, is that what's the matter?
GRANYA: (*Shouting over his head*) Watch out for Khomich. He's a squealer! I'm sure he is!
WARDRESS: Shut your face, little bitch. You'll get a rifle butt in the teeth!
(GRANYA *and* SHUROCHKA *disappear behind the side of the lorry*)

KOLODEY: Is that all?

KOSTYA: That's all.

KOLODEY: Let's have the list. (*He takes it from* KOSTYA. *To the* ESCORT-GUARD SERGEANT) Now read out the name.

ESCORT-GUARD SERGEANT: (*He has one file left in his hands*) Yevdokimov!

KOSTYA: Me? I've been posted?

ESCORT-GUARD SERGEANT: (*Shouts*) Alias . . .

KOLODEY: That's right, you've been posted. Hurry up, the escort's waiting.

ESCORT-GUARD SERGEANT: Alias . . .

KOSTYA: (*Stepping back*) Fuck you all! I won't let you take me.

POSOSHKOV: (*Stepping towards him*) Come on, Kostya, if you have to you have to.

KOSTYA: Go away, you cheap bastard! Traitor! Shit! Fuck off while you're still alive! (*He runs to one side, jumps up on the rubbish box, suddenly draws a knife and bares his stomach*) Don't come any closer! You come a step nearer, I'll rip myself up the belly!

(POSOSHKOV, AGA-MIRZA *and the wardress move towards him*)

KOSTYA: Get back! I'll carve myself up! You'll have to lug me to hospital with my guts hanging out. I'm not going!

POSOSHKOV: Kostya, please! We're your friends. It's an order—what can we do?

KOSTYA: (*Waving his knife*) You bloody son of a bitch, stinking shit-chewer, get back! So help me I'll cut your throat, then do myself in!

KOLODEY: Go on, grab him!

(*The attackers are undecided*)

AGA-MIRZA: Kostya, you're making it worse for yourself. They'll send you to a punishment camp.

KOSTYA: You lousy squealer, son of a bitch! I'm not coming. I'll rip myself up the belly!

MERESHCHUN *creeps up to* KOSTYA *from behind and strikes him a low blow under the knees.* KOSTYA *falls, they throw themselves upon him, push him to the ground, take away his knife and grip him by the throat*)

KOSTYA: (*Lying on the ground*) So you're with them too, doctor? You bum! We'll meet again and then I'll fix you!

MERESHCHUN: What do you expect? Bloody fool! If you rip your guts out, I'm the one who has to sew them back.

KOLODEY: (*To* POSOSHKOV) Get some rope.

POSOSHKOV: (*Takes some out of his pocket*) Here, I've got some, sir. Nice bit of rope, specially for the occasion, citizen commander. (*They bind* KOSTYA *hand and foot*)

KOLODEY: (*To someone*) Get his things out of the stores.

POSOSHKOV: Angel! Get his things! They're all packed and ready, sir.(ANGEL *brings in* KOSTYA's *belongings and heaves them into the back of the lorry. They push* KOSTYA *in as well, bound as he is*)

KOSTYA: Undo that bag! They're not all here! There's some missing! The bastards have stolen some of my things! My calf-skin boots! Scavengers! My leather overcoat!

KOLODEY: There's no time, the escort's waiting.

(*The back flap of the lorry is slammed shut*)

ESCORT-GUARD SERGEANT: (*In the back of the lorry*) All prisoners pay attention! Any prisoner who rises to his feet will be deemed to have attempted escape, in which case I shall open fire without warning.

(*A second machine-gunner climbs in, the lorry starts off*)

KOSTYA: (*He is invisible inside the lorry, but his shouts can be heard*) We'll meet again! I'll fix you all! You bastards, you're not through with the camps yet! I'll fix you!

AGA-MIRZA: All right, you'll fix us. We're terrified. (*The lorry departs*)

KOLODEY: (*To* POSOSHKOV) Did you take his boots?

POSOSHKOV: I've got half a suitcase full, citizen commander. There's enough for you too. It's all other people's anyway. He even pinched his officer's uniform.

KOLODEY: You're quite a boy, doctor, aren't you?

MERESHCHUN: Cheap crook! Expecting me to sew up his belly! As if I've nothing better to do. (*Walks on into his hut*)

KOLODEY: (*To the* WARDRESS *and* POSOSHKOV) Now let's frisk the prisoners. Do it properly and take your time. Watch out particularly for knives, files, vodka, letters, photos, papers with notes, any money over one hundred roubles, ink pencils . . . (*Shouts over to the check-point*) Let them in, ten at a time! (*All four of them move to the back of the stage.* ANGEL *runs up to the post and strikes the metal rail rhythmically a few times. Two check-point guards come out of their hut and stand on both sides of the parade, lanterns raised to light it. The first two files of five prisoners march in formation through the wide, opening gates*)

KOLODEY: (*Shouts*) Untie all boots and shoes! Loosen belts! (*The prisoners carry out his order. The search begins. The wind is whining.* ANGEL *walks over to the left in front of the barrack hut.* LYUBA *enters from the left, her head and body wrapped in a warm scarf. She walks past* ANGEL, *head bowed, looking at the ground*)

ANGEL: (*Calling her back*) Lyuba! You've been to the hospital? How is he? Nemov?

LYUBA: He's alive.

ANGEL: Hard nut to crack, isn't he? They won't crack that man's nut. (*He leaves. In the background the prisoners are being searched. The lanterns in the guards' hands are flickering. The fine snow is whirling. For a moment* LYUBA *does not move, then head bowed, she walks up the steps to* MERESHCHUN'*s cabin and knocks at the door.*

The door opens to let her in. One can see her shadow in the window as she takes off her scarf. The painted curtain falls)
(*It remains dark in the auditorium. The only light comes from the lanterns on the barbed wire round the orchestra pit. The sentries on the watch-towers do not move. The loudspeaker plays a tune.*

The overhead lights in the auditorium are not switched on. The ordinary curtain is not lowered)